RA D IOHEA_D

LIFE IN A GLASSHOUSE

First published in 2022 by Palazzo Editions Ltd

15 Church Road

London, SW13 9HE

www.palazzoeditions.com

Design and layout copyright © 2022 Palazzo
Editions Ltd

Text © 2022 John Aizlewood

Every effort has been made to trace and acknowledge
the copyright holders. If any unintentional omission
has occurred, we would be pleased to add an
appropriate acknowledgment in any future edition
of the book. A CIP catalogue record for this book is
available from the British Library.

ISBN 978-1-78675-034-1

eBook ISBN 978-1-78675-125-6

Manufactured in UK

10 9 8 7 6 5 4 3 2 1

Designed by Adelle Mahoney for Palazzo Editions

RA D IOHEA_D
LIFE IN A GLASSHOUSE

John Aizlewood

CONTENTS

INTRODUCTION   7

1   I WILL SING OF THE LORD'S
MERCIES FOREVER   13

2   WAITING FOR THE MAGIC   27

3   "SEE ALL YOU CREEPS THERE!"   37

4   COMING UP FOR AIR   53

5   "ONE OF THE GREATEST ALBUMS
IN LIVING MEMORY"   73

6   OK? NOT OK   91

7   EVERYTHING IN ITS RIGHT PLACE AT LAST   101

8   ROAMING IN THE GLOAMING   127

9   HOW MUCH WOULD YOU LIKE TO PAY, SIR?   143

10   LET'S TAKE OUR TIME   155

11   A SORROW SHAPED HOLE   165

12   WE HAVE BECOME VERY ADEPT AT
BEING RADIOHEAD   177

ACKNOWLEDGMENTS, SOURCES AND
PICTURE CREDITS   192

INTRODUCTION

How do you do it? How do you become global pop superstars? Deep down, nobody really knows. There are harder questions still: having reached the summit, what next? How do you avoid musical stagnation and the temptation to endlessly recycle whatever it was that got you there in the first place? And since it's not just about the music (how can it be?), how do you resist the usual temptations of life in a glasshouse: creative inertia, drink, drugs, fractured relationships inside and outside the mothership, and, the biggest usurpers of all, hubris and self-indulgence? It isn't easy. It's not meant to be easy.

Radiohead wouldn't admit to being capable of offering an answer to any of those questions. Until recently, they wouldn't even admit to looking back, but no band has done it like they have. They cracked a code which had hitherto thwarted everyone, only for "everyone" to discover that the code they'd cracked applied to Radiohead and Radiohead alone. Bucking any known trend, they have become more popular as their music has become both more extreme (possibly) and less compromising (undoubtedly). Here they are, over three decades on from a genesis that was as mundane as a bar band, jaw-droppingly popular wherever they look, having changed names (albeit just the once) more often than personnel and management, but less—much less—than they have changed musical and career course. As that overfamiliar song tells us, they've done it their way, but it's been a curious, contradictory mélange of stubbornness, farsighted planning, spontaneous decision-making, bravery, inspiration, more stubbornness, luck, wit, blind faith, incendiary live performances, yet more stubborn-ness, and a creative well from which they draw deeper as the years roll on. Those who live in glasshouses aren't supposed to throw stones, but Radiohead come armed with buckets of boulders. How do you do it? Not like this, surely.

Individually, they're the sort of characters you'd find in any band from The Beatles to One Direction. There's the hypochondriac benign dictator, the gregarious one, the quiet one, the enigmatic one, and the muso. As their mothers might say, they are special in their own ways. Yet put these stereotypes from central casting together in a studio or on a stage and each transforms into some kind of shaman, and a unique magic emerges, a whole infinitely greater than the sum of each crucial part.

Not for Colin Greenwood, his younger brother Jonny, Ed O'Brien, Phil Selway, and Thom Yorke the hardscrabble upbringing and/or the heartache of fractious families, that often spawn major musical talent, although the Greenwoods' father died when they were young and Ed is from what used to be called a broken home. Instead, they met at the fee-paying Abingdon School close to the banks of the River Thames in Oxfordshire, and the closest they seem to have come to parents-off-spring disharmony is the almost imperceptibly raised eyebrows of the Greenwood family when Jonny quit his music degree, an exit, lest we forget, which came with the blessing of his tutor.

They formed at school, so they must have been close friends, yes? No. They were acquaintances, brought together by a great liking of music rather than any great liking of each other, but that would come. They would be kept together by music and an increased mutual understand-ing. They don't like to talk about intra-band feelings, but in March 2019, this least rock 'n' roll of institutions was inducted into the Rock and Roll Hall of Fame. In his acceptance speech, with Phil stood beside him, gui-tarist Ed explained why they are who they are:

My biggest thank you is for my brothers, Thom, Colin and Johnny. I want to thank them for their integrity, their authenticity, their commitment. None of these things you should take for granted. I also want to thank them for the musicians they are, for that thing when we play together; that collective sound we make; for some of the nights in the rehearsal studio which are transcendental moments. But most of all, I want to thank them for this deep, deep friendship. We couldn't have done this without this love for one another. There's such a deep, deep bond and it's a beautiful thing. So thank you. I love you.

So, while it's always been about, yes, the music, this hermetically sealed collective see the bigger picture too. They had the poise to postpone a full immersion into that music of theirs while four of them completed their education at separate locations, distant from their Oxford lair. This deferred gratification took place without so much as a flicker of unrest or the suggestion that any of these very different characters would be seduced by academia, girls, a proper job, the urge not to return to base camp, or that serial killer of school bands, maturity. They left Oxford. They passed their degrees. They returned to Oxford. They took on the world. Such discipline was (and remains) remarkable and not just for a bunch of bright teenagers. Alas, it was the only remarkable thing about the band then named On A Friday.

Not for them, a protracted, dues-paying apprenticeship or the logical stepping-stones of album-by-album career progression (REO Speedwagon took seven almost identical, major label albums to breach the US Top 30). Instead, Radiohead build things up and then they tear them down, usually while tearing their hair out. When they make albums, it's mostly a ludicrously lengthy, often painful, always self-questioning, self-flagellating process, interspersed with moments of joy and revelation. It always ends in something truly special. Crucially, with one glaring exception, each album has been a musically violent reaction to its predecessor.

Admirably unconcerned with the circular firing squad that was indie credibility, On A Friday were quickly signed by a major label. From Parlophone's point of view, rather than being inspired by a fervid belief in their new charges, the signing was more a bet-hedging exercise from the label of Bliss and Escape Club as much as Paul McCartney and Pet Shop Boys. Unsurprisingly, label and band jostled for career hegemony and the swiftly rechristened Radiohead's genius emerged slowly.

They introduced themselves to the world's charts with a career-threatening fluke. The always out of context "Creep" seemed likely to be as fleeting a success as OMC's "How Bizarre," Wheatus' lyrically similar "Teenage Dirtbag," and countless other here-today-"barbecue-sauce-with-your-pizza-sir?"-tomorrow flashes in the pan. "Creep" made and almost destroyed Radiohead. Weighed down by The Hit and some inferior ballast, the first album, 1993's *Pablo Honey*, was almost universally reviewed as fairly promising, but very flawed. It's an assessment hindsight has done little to alter.

They couldn't and wouldn't make "Creep II," so that ought to have been that. Sometimes the band thought so too, but 1995's *The Bends* was an artistic rebirth, and its towering 1997 successor, *OK Computer*, is one of the great albums in popular music. They had reached the summit.

-

Received wisdom has it that Radiohead were blinded by the view from that summit and went weird. They didn't: they had a hunch that they could loiter on said summit without destroying themselves and they ran with it. True, 2000's magnificent *Kid A* might have been the most awkward, angular album to top both the British and American charts (it was unquestionably the bravest), but, as we now know, it was Radiohead being Radiohead and restarting from scratch.

Following 2001's *Amnesiac* came consolidation, or, more accurately, commercial consolidation. For all the band's myriad insecurities, a fanatical, ever-growing fan base means they are secure in their status, for, make no mistake, Radiohead always want to sell records. Always. That fan base embraces change and therefore it allows the band the freedom to do as they will. It's a precious gift which Radiohead instinctively understand. Like the smartest characters in any fairy tale, they use what they have been given wisely.

Base and fan base secured, they embarked upon the momentous musical journey that would be 2003's *Hail to the Thief*, 2007's *In Rainbows*, 2011's *The King of Limbs*, 2016's *A Moon Shaped Pool*, the remarkable live album of 2001, *I Might Be Wrong: Live Recordings*, plus assorted solo endeavors. It's never been clear what Radiohead are going to do next, but it is clear they have got it right, just about every time. *Life in a Glasshouse* is their story.

The Headless Chickens days.

1
I WILL SING OF THE LORD'S MERCIES FOREVER

Stereotyping the British isn't as easy as it sometimes looks. They don't all love to queue. They don't all prefer their fish fried, encased in something called "batter," accompanied by something that claims to be "chips" and, if you're really blessed, something that thinks it's "mushy" peas. They're not all criminal masterminds with a Jeremy Irons accent. And the population is no more comprised of Dickensian urchins than it is of bowler-hatted toffs.

One thing does remain stereotypically British though: the ability to place someone socially from the school they attended. Schools are either state (i.e. funded by the government and available to all); private (i.e. funded by parents and for the well-off); or public, which aren't actually for the public, but which form the top tier of the privately funded school network: they are for the very well-off.

Let's look at one school in particular: Abingdon School, a private educational establishment for boys aged between eleven and eighteen. Like many British schools it was founded by monks, probably long before the official starting date of 1256. It is the sort of school that is beyond the financial reach of the overwhelming majority of British people, but not, by any means, everyone. Located in the small town of Abingdon, six miles south of Oxford, Abingdon School is a place of timeless beauty, which prides itself on academic achievement and molding the boy into a man: "Our aim," claims its mission statement, "is to ensure each boy thrives at Abingdon and, through challenge and opportunity, achieves the most from his potential."

Achievement doesn't come cheap. In 2019–20, the cost for parents of pupils who reside there seven days a week is £41,145 a year. For local day boys, the rate drops to a less punishing (but still hefty) £20,655.

As befits an establishment whose outward appearance has barely changed since it moved to its current location in 1870, Abingdon's history is rich and varied. As early as the sixteenth century, alongside the usual private school mixture of minor bishops and mediocre MPs, it produced a composer, John Bennet, who wrote madrigals for Queen Elizabeth I. More recent alumni include Matthew Harding, the insurance magnate who saved the financially stricken Chelsea Football Club in 1993; comedian David Mitchell; Tom Hollander, one of those 'I've seen his face but I can't remember his name' actors; and day boys Colin Charles Greenwood, Jonathan Richard Guy Greenwood, Edward John O'Brien, Philip James Selway, and Thomas Edward Yorke, five locals collectively and rather better known as Radiohead.

Thom and Colin were in the same year, gazed upon with a certain aloof superiority by Ed and Phil, who were, respectively, one and two school years older and therefore the very acme of sophistication. Little Jonny Greenwood was a whole three years beneath Thom and Colin. The Greenwoods' always cordial relations were best maintained if Jonny kept out of Colin's way at school.

At Abingdon there would be kinship between the day boys, as there was between the weekday and weekly boarders, but friendship groups among eleven-year-old boys are flickering and fleeting. All the same, Thom, Colin, and Ed slowly converged. By 1982 the punk revolution had come and gone, but unsurprisingly, despite a certain commitment to the arts, Abingdon School was not at the forefront of contemporary musical developments, and so, rather like Iron Age men who still worked with bronze, it had eventually spawned a punk band, TNT. They weren't very good, but Colin was a member and so too was Thom. It was the sort of band where nobody wanted to sing, so Thom had a go. Then he left. Doggedly, Colin stayed on and Thom felt sufficiently guilty to continue their musical link.

Meanwhile, Ed and Colin had discovered each other when they co-starred in a school performance of Gilbert and Sullivan's whimsical marital farce, *Trial by Jury*. The circle was complete in November 1984, when the pair moved on to a modernized version of *A Midsummer Night's Dream* and Thom provided experimental (i.e. un-listenable) musical accompaniment. Thom thought Ed was "cool" and looked like then-revered Smiths singer Morrissey and so the pair were invited to join the band Thom was secretly recruiting. The threesome wore berets, catsuits, blouses, and, in heavily made-up Thom's case, a crushed velvet dinner suit. Needless to say, the school's sporting curriculum was not a high priority for these fops.

The boys were of an artistic bent, but they were hardly maverick material. Like most teenage boys, Thom thought he didn't fit in. He was born on October 7, 1968 in Wellingborough, a sleepy market town in Northamptonshire, middle England both spiritually and geographically. According to Thom, his father, Graham, had been a nuclear physicist who'd studied at Imperial College London, but now, he sold chemical engineering equipment. When Thom was just two months old, the Yorkes moved north to Lundin Links, a small village on the north shore of the Firth of Forth, on the east coast of Scotland. "I'd go down to the beach every day," he told the *Daily Record*. "All I remember is the incredible brightness."

In truth, brightness was an issue for Thom throughout his childhood. At birth, both his eyes were closed and his left one was paralyzed. Five operations later, the little chap was still only six years old, and once the surgeons had grafted a piece of buttock muscle onto his eyelid, their work was as done as it could be. He was left with a droopy eyelid (one more operation would have corrected the droop, but kept the eye permanently open: Thom demurred) and the realization that he would never be a pilot.

There were other legacies too: the red Adidas tracksuit with which his parents had bought his acquiescence to surgery and which he wore until he outgrew it; the vomiting sessions and narcotic dreams induced by general anesthetic; the sound of wheezing from the geriatric ward along the corridor. Television was inappropriate for a boy with eye troubles, so his hospital stays were soundtracked by the radio and visualized by his imagination. No wonder he'd have an on-off medical fixation ("Bones," "My Iron Lung") when he found his vocation. Oh, and his father had some lessons to impart: "He taught me to be very suspicious of people, not to trust anyone. I really had to unlearn that. It's much better to attempt to trust people until they prove you wrong."

Music wasn't a big priority. The family's only hi-fi was in their Volvo car, and the most played cassette was a traditional Scottish dance compilation. When Thom was nine, the Yorkes moved again, this time to Witney, ten miles north-west of Oxford, where they would finally settle. Thom was dispatched to Standlake, the local (state) primary school where his mother, Barbara, secured a job as a teacher. Thom wore the regulation blue pullover with a certain amount of pride and his eye-patch with a certain amount of embarrassment. As a Church of England school, its stated core values—thankfulness, honesty, love, tolerance, compassion, and forgiveness—are underpinned by Christian principles, and while Radiohead have railed against many sacred cows since, Christianity has stayed out of their firing line.

Christian or not, kids will be kids and a scrawny boy with an eye-patch and an alien accent inherited from his Scottish years might as well have had a target on his back. "I was," he confessed to *Vox*, "starting to become more self-conscious." That self-consciousness would never disappear. Years later, he could handle stadium crowds, yet queuing in a bank would induce a panic attack. All the same, childhood was a sunny place: "My mother always said I was a quiet and happy kid," he told *Q*. "I didn't get kicked around. Sorry to disappoint."

Thom's father had been a boxer at university. He bought his son boxing gloves and administered a few lessons in the noble art. Hyperactive as he was, Thom had no problems in scrapping with his tormenters, but he did have problems learning to box. The gloves were abandoned; the fighting was not.

A former art student who loved trad jazz, Barbara Yorke was a lover not a fighter, and for Thom's eighth birthday she bought her son a Spanish guitar. He was obsessed with Lego; with a book about Bridges, by educational publishers Ladybird ("The Gladesville Bridge is a very fine, modern bridge. Steel rods in the concrete give it extra strength."); with dismantling electric goods; and with solo bicycle trips to nearby gravel pits, where he would practice stunts, left eye notwithstanding. Ever game, he not only had a bash at that Spanish guitar, but he built another himself, in honor of that noted guitar builder Brian May of Queen, whose parts on "Bohemian Rhapsody" Thom attempted to emulate. Eventually, he managed to crank out something which vaguely approximated to "Kum Ba Yah," the spiritual he had discovered at school assemblies.

If Standlake represented Thom's innocence, Abingdon, which he entered in 1980, was its crushing end. Slowly, music began to envelop him: "The music room and art department was my sanctuary from a posh private boys' school full of arseholes: I don't blend well." Before he met Colin and Ed, he'd written his first song as an eleven-year-old (about a nuclear bomb; of course it was about a nuclear bomb), and he had been in a band of sorts, an unnamed duo where Thom would play rudimentary guitar, while a long-lost friend would add electronic sounds taken from recordings of television programs. He became acquainted with

Queen's *Greatest Hits*, the first of Thom's cassettes to be played in the latest Volvo (Volvo followed Volvo in the Yorke family), and then *A Night at the Opera* (i.e. the one which included the "Paranoid Android" template, Thom's beloved "Bohemian Rhapsody"), but still guitar proficiency remained elusive.

And then there was the other side of school, the social side. Day boys were bottom of the Abingdon food chain, and the day boy with the wonky eye was bottom of the bottom of the chain. They called that boy Salamander and as adolescence kicked in with its spots, its varying voice, its life dedicated to Onan, and its desperate awkwardness with girls, the boy went feral for a while. Admittedly, it was feral by the standards of the fairly privileged, but between the ages of thirteen and fifteen, Dodo, as his younger brother Andy nicknamed him, went off the rails for the first time, spending hour after Freudian hour underneath (he claims) a poster of a Volvo 244DL's crumple zones, making music in the room above his parents' television room. "I drove my parents mad, I don't know how they put up with it, but they were pretty tolerant," he told Radio 1 in 2019. "Now I live in a house with two children and they're doing exactly the same thing to me."

Much as he chafed against his guitar and singing lessons, music was Thom's anchor. The kid who'd loved the sweetness of The Beatles became the youth who was obsessed by Joy Division and Magazine, the darkness on the edge of town where Joy Division's Ian Curtis essentially outlined his plans for suicide via his lyrics and Magazine's Howard Devoto threatened, rather ungallantly all things considered, to "drug you and fuck you on the permafrost."

But there was more. Behind their leaders, Joy Division and fellow Mancunians Magazine crafted extraordinary backdrops. Joy Division evoked a Manchester that was both space age and drenched in sepulchral Victorian gloom, while Magazine were clearly more familiar with the

Krautrockers of Faust and Can than they were with bog-standard indie: everything would change for Thom, but not his understanding and adoration of this. Anyway, when fourteen-year-old Thom joined TNT, to the delight of his perma-worried mother, he knuckled down at school too. He won a prize for music, although he couldn't read music. ("I tried and tried and tried and still can't.") He won a prize for art, although he couldn't really paint.

His first concert was Joan Armatrading—he loved her deep, vulnerable voice—at Oxford Apollo in 1983, but more pivotal was seeing Siouxsie and the Banshees at the same venue two years later, when the singer's broken leg forced her to sit down without losing her natural authority. A few weeks later, a grumpy New Order—Joy Division post the deceased Ian Curtis—showed him how not to do it.

While Thom was a little ball of pent-up frustration, Colin was a cheery boy, despite being teased for the shape of his head. More seriously, the good nature of the man Ed still calls "Cozzie" survived the death of his father, Raymond, an army bomb disposal expert, when he was seven. Born on June 26, 1969 at the John Radcliffe Infirmary, Oxford, his family soon moved to Germany, to Didcot, to Suffolk, to Abingdon, before settling in the village of Oakley. His parents loved Simon & Garfunkel, Scott Joplin, and Mozart and they bought him a guitar for his seventh birthday. He took guitar lessons at school, but there was a teacher—there's always a teacher—who opened his eyes. Terence Gilmore-James had instructed him in classical guitar, but Abingdon's director of music opened Colin and the rest of the band's ears to the jazz of Miles Davis, the film soundtracks of Bernard Herrmann, and the contemporary classical music of Krzysztof Penderecki, all of whom would loom large in Radiohead's future world.

Colin would stroll into his exams, nerves soothed by listening to R.E.M.'s *Reckoning* on his Walkman, and, later, when things became fractious within the band on the road, he could be found drinking with the road crew, seemingly without a care in the world. His older sister, Susan, introduced him (and, by osmosis, Thom and Jonny) to Magazine. Thom was enraptured, but Colin was obsessed and seeds were already being sown. Years later, *The New Yorker* would expand: "Colin is easily distracted and delighted by the world around him, favoring the words "mad," "brilliant," and "amazing," the last spoken with a long, liquid stress on the second syllable. He has a habit of suddenly burying his face in his hands as if he were sinking into despair, or falling asleep; after a moment, his face lights up again."

Ed O'Brien, the cabal's third member, was born on April 15, 1968 in Oxford. One grandfather hailed from Tipperary, while another was an ornithologist who gave Ed a lifelong love of birds and birdsong. His father, John, was a music maven, rather more in touch with the cutting edge than might be expected of a well-to-do chiropractor. When his parents split up, ten-year-old Ed lived with his mother, Eve. He'd later switch parents, while keeping fond relations with both. When he took up the guitar, after spells playing trumpet and trombone in the school orchestra, there was only encouragement at home. "He brings us extra sounds," says Thom of the man whose primary influence is jazz renegade John McLaughlin and whose favorite album is Marvin Gaye's *What's Going On*.

The trio were less encouraged in their quest for musical salvation by the school's headmaster from 1975 to 2001, Michael St. John Parker, who, despite the school's motto declaring "I will sing of the Lord's mercies forever" and the opposition of the head of music, banned this new-fangled pop music from school grounds after a punk gig where townies turned up and slashed the new arts theater's seats. Never the least eccentric man in any room, without succumbing to such practicalities as ordination, the son of a reverend dressed as a bishop and gave sermons to his captive audience. Later, "Bishop's Robes" would tell the tale in some detail. "He was one fucked up guy, an evil petty little man and I still hate him," admitted Thom, long after it should have mattered.

Undeterred by peculiar headmasters and looming exams, in 1985 the trio formed a band, called themselves Shindig, then Dearest, then Gravitate, and finally On A Friday after their rehearsal night. They recruited a fourth member in the shape of a pliant but unreliable drum machine (very) loosely modeled on Sisters Of Mercy's Doktor Avalanche. The world beckoned, or, more accurately, some pubs in Oxford beckoned. The very early gigs were "a bit pants," admitted Thom.

Unquestioning, but short on ideas and personality, the drum machine was swiftly jettisoned. Having made the decision, On A Friday didn't know what to do with it, establishing a template for the next thirty-something years. Making decisions was always relatively easy; following up with an alternative plan much less so. Another local band, Jungle Telegraph, covered U.K. Subs tunes and were as unappealing as their name, except for their drummer. Phil Selway was born in Hemingford Grey, Cambridgeshire—former home of former British prime minister John Major—on May 23, 1967, when *More of the Monkees* topped the American and British charts. His parents, Michael and Dorothea, purchased a drum kit for his third Christmas, and at Abingdon he studied classical percussion. A wry but placid young man with a teeth-rotting sweet habit, Jungle Telegraph's drummer still wasn't wholly sure he wasn't really a guitarist. Nevertheless, a seduction of the older boy was planned, but peculiarly, when that seduction attempt was made, it was made without On A Friday's most appealing member, Colin. Nevertheless, Phil acquiesced, although someone who admired the combative Stewart Copeland's under-acknowledged contribution to The Police really could have done without Thom berating him at his first rehearsal: "Can't you play any fucking faster?" Later Thom would laud Phil for bringing "feel" to Radiohead.

Those early days were a fumbling mess. Thom's parents would drive him to gigs sometimes, but they disapproved of this music malarkey and so he pretended he was having sleepovers when gig nights became more frequent. Parental disapproval would have been expressed more vehemently still had they heard Thom's improvised version of Siouxsie and the Banshees' cover of The Beatles' "Dear Prudence," which was aired at the band's first school show, or other early songs such as "The Chains," with its Celtic viola, and "Rattlesnake," which married Thom's distorted vocals with a drum loop. Discerning ears recommended divorce, but "Rattlesnake" was a gateway to a distant future.

Things were evolving but not gelling. Colin had a color-blind kid brother, Jonny (or as Colin, but nobody else, has it, Jonathan), who was born in Oxford on November 5, 1971, when John Lennon's *Imagine* topped the British and American album charts. Jonny was as shy and reserved as Colin wasn't, but the brothers got on so well they were nicknamed the sisters. He too had absorbed Magazine via their sister, Susan (who would become a computer consultant and magazine shop owner in Bath), but being seven or eight and having been gifted a recorder when Colin had his first guitar, he picked up on the sound of John McGeogh's inventive guitars rather than Howard Devoto's lyrics. Having been introduced to musicals, Simon & Garfunkel, and the brass-led parts of Mozart by his mother, Jonny's tastes were more poppy, so the first single he purchased was the pink vinyl version of Squeeze's "Cool For Cats." The innuendos ("I'm invited in for coffee and I give the dog a bone") sailed over his head, but the melody did not.

Oh, and Jonny was a mostly self-taught musical prodigy who played with the Thames Vale Youth Orchestra, flitting between guitar, viola, violin, recorder, and piano. When he messed about, he messed about with a Rickenbacker and some effects pedals. Aged fifteen and under the inspirational sway of Terence Gilmore-James, he discovered the ondes Martenot, the musical instrument that is part-electronic-organ, part-theremin. It was invented in 1928 by French cellist Maurice Martenot, and as featured on Olivier Messiaen's *Turangalîla-Symphonie* (Jonny's favorite piece of music) and the *Star Trek* theme. Already an adroit computer programmer, Jonny discovered angular indie titans The Fall and their splendidly curmudgeonly singer, Mark E. Smith. Things were never quite the same again: "Mark E. Smith was completely the voice of my teenage years. More than any other singer, easily. When I think of myself in my bedroom, he's there, talking or ranting through something."

During a life which, according to Thom, is "dedicated to searching for the notes and sounds you shouldn't use," Jonny would take to kite-flying, develop an obsession with camp 1960s British radio comedy *Round the Horne*, indulge in the "mental masturbation" of fiendishly difficult crosswords, and quote Philip Larkin on "The Lozenge of Love." There would be psychoactive drugs, but he claims, just the once; his manager talked him down. There wouldn't, he maintains, be groupies: "It's treating sex like sneezing."

So, on the one hand, Jonny was the sort of kid you'd want in your struggling band, and in fact he was actually in one, Illiterate Hands, with Andy Yorke. On the other, the kid in question was Colin's kid brother and who wants one of those in their band? Kids, eh?

On A Friday hedged their bets and allowed little Jonny to hang out during rehearsals, occasionally playing another of his instruments, the harmonica. A blind man could have seen the writing on the wall when they acquired keyboards with the express wish of sounding more like Talking Heads. Needless to say, as a keyboards player whose favorite bands included Talking Heads, Jonny was delighted.

On a Monday, August 4, 1986, at the Jericho Tavern, Oxford's premier venue for local and national independent bands, On A Friday played their first show that wasn't for schoolmates. Members of the Jericho's Club Avocado paid £1; non-members £1.50 with membership generously thrown in. Radiohead legend has it that nearly-fifteen-year-old Jonny was sitting in the wings ("wings" is coating the 120-capacity Jericho with a grandeur it never had, but he was next to the stage) caressing his harmonica when Thom summoned him onto the stage. The quintet was still not formally complete. Jonny would be kept waiting until February 1988 to become a full member, albeit a full member mostly exiled to keyboards and harmonica. Again, the world beckoned. Except that, again, it didn't really.

"My mother always said I was a quiet and happy kid. I didn't get kicked around. Sorry to disappoint." THOM

Thom and Colin's kid brother, Jonny. Early days.

2
WAITING FOR THE MAGIC

G ood, middle-class, well-educated British boys are inculcated with certain noble values. Those noble values don't include their parents sanctioning their departure from expensive education at sixteen or eighteen. This means going to university, preferably a good one, rather than something that includes the phrase "further education" in its title. It most assuredly did not mean hanging around among Oxford's 120,000 population ("It's crawling with pretentious wankers," snapped Thom), playing in some tinpot local band while observing the students who would one day rule the land gallivanting around town.

Oxford is not like an American college town (to pluck one out of the air, Athens, GA) where the student population drags the natives towards coffee-shop bohemia. Oxford students, those future rulers, tend not to live in neighborhoods such as Blackbird Leys, which are as deprived as any in Britain. Neither did Radiohead. And when Phil, the oldest member, sailed through his A levels and secured a place to read English and History at Liverpool Polytechnic, 169 miles from Oxford, he went. Of course he went, that's what Abingdon School boys did.

Phil kept drumming, most notably in the student version of *Return to the Forbidden Planet*. He also became a volunteer for Samaritans, the British charity which provides emotional support, usually via telephone, for people contemplating suicide. It's a complicated role which requires deep reservoirs of tact and empathy. Radiohead's success would eventually mean he couldn't offer the time commitment required, but his future wife, Cait, would manage the Oxford branch and Phil would run the 2002

London Marathon for them, in just over the four hours he'd hoped for. As he told *The Irish Times* in 2010, "I sincerely hope it's something I can return to in later life." After graduating, he would return to Oxford and take a post-grad course in publishing.

The band made their first demo tape of six tracks in February 1987 (Thom was too shy to put his name to it, so it was sent under Ed's; a song called "Fat Girl" wasn't a good idea, even then; although their first review, by Dave Newton of the *Oxford Enquirer*, decided they were "a band worth hearing") and a stodgy fourteen-song follow-up later that year. They included two saxophone-playing sisters who responded to hecklers with the internationally recognized hand signal for masturbation. "We were young men from a boys' school, so of course it was exciting," remembered Phil decades later of this rare connection with the opposite sex.

All the same, On A Friday were offered a tentative deal by Island. Showing a sagacity beyond both their tender years and their vaunting ambition, they admitted they weren't ready and turned it down. Anyway, they had degrees to get.

After a year off, Ed headed north to study economics at the University of Manchester, 161 miles from Oxford but much closer to Old Trafford, home of his soccer team, Manchester United. Blessed with what Phil describes as a "hard-bitten intellect," Colin went to study English at Cambridge, one of the world's foremost universities and, like Oxford, an incubator for the nation's very brightest. Being unassuming almost cost Colin his place, for Abingdon were slugabeds in spotting his potential.

No matter, Colin enrolled at Cambridge's oldest college, Peterhouse, which had deigned to admit female students as recently as 1985. He would become the college's Entertainments Officer and among the bands the scamp booked was one from Oxford called On A Friday. His thesis was on Raymond Carver, the hard-living, hard-drinking king of the American short story. Unlike his bandmates, Colin would keep his academic hand in. In 2004, he agreed to join the judging panel of the prestigious Arts Council-funded Next Generation Poets competition, where several young poets are anointed as Britain's best. Chairman of the judges and future Poet Laureate Simon Armitage commended Colin's contribution as "softly spoken and thoughtful."

To this day Colin still dreams of a return: "I entertain this fantasy of going back to college, being this Sterling Morrison-like figure clutching onto academic respectability after the ephemeral respectability of pop music."

Not for the first or last time, Thom was in tune with the others, while not being like them. "I had a very expensive education," he told *New Musical Express* in 2001. "It took me years to come to terms with that. A long, long, long time." He joined the real world, taking a gap year in Oxford: "I wanted to discover if I was completely insane and if I really wanted to be a musician or not." Predictably, Thom and the real world was not a meeting of minds. He batted aside his father's attempts to get him to take a job in advertising, the language of which he would later subvert in a succession of Radiohead sleeves. There was a bad romance with too many public spats during which she would sometimes call him a creep. Hair long and dyed blond in honor of Japan's David Sylvian, Thom worked at Cult, a gentlemen's clothing emporium, selling suits. Badly. He'd later claim it was the department store Debenhams. His boss replaced Michael St. John Parker as a hate figure, being "one of those blokes who'd drive to work, kill a cyclist and not stop." Not always one for the general public, although even in his darkest days he was always a diplomatic delight with fans who wanted a conversation (never to be confused with a conversation about "Creep"), he tried bar work with similar results. Only a stint as an orderly at a mental hospital proved successful, chiefly because it offered fertile songwriting ground.

Nature took its course, and in 1988, Thom enrolled at the University of Exeter, 154 miles from Oxford, to study Fine Art and Literature. "I could never work out how I blagged my way into college," he claimed, disingenuously. Apart from being beaten up by townies, because (he maintained) he dressed like an old man on one of his many people-watching expeditions outside the Devon city's Guildhall Shopping Centre, Thom had a ball at a university which, for all its academic prestige, was not short of outsiders like (but not really like) himself.

In his first year, he immersed himself in the student drinking culture, unconvincingly claiming that "I almost died from alcohol poisoning," before, as he had at Abingdon, getting a grip and knuckling down once he'd discovered computer art. He also developed an interest in outsider art, including that by the pedophile who would inspire the On A Friday song "Nothing Touches Me," but he wisely retreated on discovering just what a freakshow the whole outsider art circus was.

There were student bands too. Thom's blond locks were swapped for a shaved head. He became a successful student DJ and so began to buy singles for the first time. "Being a DJ meant I could be in a room without having to talk to people and it was an excuse to spend loads of money on records and be a cult figure," he admitted. "It was great for my ego. I wasn't particularly good, because people bought me drinks to get me to play what they wanted. At the end of the night, I couldn't see the records." He joined Flickernoise, who sported dreadlocks and played hardcore house before the genre had been invented: another musical seed was sown. There was the more conventional Headless (formerly Headless Chicken), who'd do a passable version of Prince's "Raspberry Beret" and one of Thom's songs, "High & Dry." There was even a surprisingly accomplished single, the turbo-charged "I Don't Want to Go to Woodstock," with a violin solo from John Matthias. Thom's backing vocals were enjoyably reminiscent of The Stranglers' "Duchess."

Most important of all, in 1990 he met Rachel Owen, the woman with whom he'd share his life with for the next twenty-three years. A student of Italian and Fine Art (Painting) from Cardiff, she introduced him to the work of Scottish painter Alan Davie; she was beautiful; she was super-bright, even in comparison to Thom; and she was laudably sensible. What, therefore, she was doing with Thom wasn't entirely clear, but as influences go there would be none more benign outside his bandmates. "I pursued her because I was terrified of her," he told *Vox*. "She thought I was a freak: moody, difficult, unpleasant and idiotic. I was, but she bashed a lot of that crap out of me." Having told *Rolling Stone* "I masturbate a lot; I haven't met a beautiful woman I've liked," there was much crap to lose.

And what of Jonny, behind the rest as ever? For all his musical brilliance he was still far from adept on keyboards, while his harmonica enhanced nothing. As the last member to join On A Friday, he feared he would be first to leave in the event of a cull. His insecurity revealed itself when he began his degree in Music and Psychology. Rather than leave town, he chose to study at Oxford Polytechnic, or Oxford Brookes University as it was rechristened in 1992, the educational equivalent of a supermarket generic brand. He could have done better, but he saw and sought the future.

After just three months, Jonny dropped out. His mother, Brenda, being his mother, was upset, but he went with the blessing of his tutor, the first Radiohead educator to see the bigger picture since the admirable Terence Gilmore-James.

The history of pop music is littered with local bands comprised of bright boys who went to university. We don't know their names because they don't count, they're not meant to count. You dabble away in your local band, maybe becoming a minor local celebrity, while embarking upon your first fairly serious romantic relationship, promising, of course, to remain true for the next three/four years of separation. At university the outside world intrudes. You become a student; you embark upon your first very serious relationship (having dumped your local amour four days after their awkward sole visit) and you make a whole new circle of friends, before getting a degree, a job and a home that's anywhere but in your hometown. Local band? What local band?

There's a second scenario for those who're really serious about their music. They make vague promises about keeping the local band going, but at university they meet like-minded souls, more emotionally and musically developed than those left behind. A university band is formed, named (plucking a name out of the air: Coldplay) and, in the unlikely event members don't disperse forever after graduation, they pursue their calling at a higher level while using their first local band as amusing fodder during interviews to show how far they've progressed.

Not On A Friday. They all went to higher education and, Jonny excepted, they all completed their degrees. And, as if they were wearing musical pledge rings, they remained true to each other. They returned to Oxford most weekends; they returned to Oxford for most of every summer, although the summer Phil spent in Bangor, Northern Ireland pursuing a woman whom he thought was the love of his life is rarely spoken of. On completing their degrees, they had letters after their names, but it was as if they'd never been away. Something that never happens, actually happened: they all returned home to finish what they started. The student years were fun though.

The university hiatus saw the students blossom as people and as intellects, but, against overwhelming odds, the chains that bound them had held. They had discovered American alternative music, most zealously Oxford-anchored Jonny, whose affection for Dinosaur Jr.'s guitar pioneer J. Mascis would never fade. On A Friday had blossomed too; they were minor players on the Oxford scene, which itself was a minor branch of the indie tree. But something kept them together, even if it was such lumpen tunes as "Jerusalem" and "Everybody Lies Through Their Teeth," portraits of their hometown which confirmed that what kept them together wasn't Oxford itself.

By the summer of 1991, the boys were back in town and their parents weren't there to be sponged off. Thom took a job in an architect's office and started writing with Jonny. The pair immersed themselves in Lou Reed's *New York* album, while anointing Pixies as "the best band ever, ever, ever." Ahead of his role as Radiohead's public relations arm, Ed toured the US on a Greyhound bus and drifted between stints as a ponytailed waiter at the ultra-hip Browns restaurant on Woodstock Road (some of the female clientele popped in at the Jericho to check out Ed's other job) and the less inevitable photographer's assistant.

Phil was the most practical, of course. He taught English to foreign students and supported his post-grad course with a stint as a subeditor at a medical publisher. Much to the envy of the others who weren't Phil, and much to the further disappointment of Mrs. Greenwood ("She's not happy unless she's worrying; very Radiohead that," noted Colin), her eldest son bagged himself a job at the Westgate Centre branch of record store chain Our Price. Less cutting edge than other national chains Virgin and HMV, one aspect of Oxford Our Price would change the lives of Colin and his bandmates forever: it was a regular haunt of record company sales reps, looking to place stock and perhaps secure a window display too.

On A Friday rang the changes too. The saxy sisters were dumped (Phil remains in contact with one of them, Charlotte) as was their usual encore, an appropriately pumped-up version of Elvis Costello and the Attractions' "Pump It Up." They busked in Oxford city center, and local heroes Ride enjoyed their version of an R.E.M. song nobody can quite remember. That spring, they made another demo tape, this time at Oxford's Dungeon Studio. "Stop Whispering" was there, alongside "What Is It That You Say" and "Give It Up." Ed took over management duties and when they played their first gig since their return, at West Oxford's Holly Bush on July 22, 1991, Jonny was on guitar as well as keyboards. An EMI A&R man was there to see it. He passed.

Relationships were strengthened by endless communal coffees in the basement of Oxford's Museum of Modern Art and, undeterred by the horrors of the communal student life they'd already experienced, like a more childish *The Young Ones*, On A Friday moved in together in a semi-detached student house on Ridgefield Road on the south-east edge of Oxford city center. "We weren't mates," stressed Ed, "we were co-conspirators." Five soon became four. Phil quickly decided that the squalor, the disorganization, Colin's obsession with indie also-rans Pale Saints and Thom's with hardcore house, not to mention the pesto slop which passed for food at almost every meal, were not for him. Striking a bold blow for decency, Phil moved out. "Jonny never did the washing up," lamented Colin and by the end of their year's lease only Thom and Colin remained.

Yet, the tribal drums had been beating. Something was afoot. The Dungeon demo tape including "Stop Whispering" had made the rounds, reaching, among others, Chris Hufford, Oxford's version of Sam Phillips crossed with 'Colonel' Tom Parker. On August 8, 1991, On A Friday played the Jericho Tavern. Afterwards, Hufford made his way backstage. "He was almost shaking," remembered Colin to *Vox*. "He said we were the best band he'd seen in three years."

In the mid-eighties, Aerial FX weren't much of a band, even by Oxford standards, but they briefly signed to EMI. When the inevitable happened after their pop-synth album *Watching the Dance* tanked, vocalist Chris Hufford and keyboardist Bryce Edge returned home to lick their wounds and invest in real estate. Their first attempt at property speculation was a development named Georgetown, in the village of Sutton Courtenay, two miles south of Abingdon School. Part of the project was a recording studio which the new owners allowed Chris Hufford and Bryce Edge to rent. The pair established a venue where local bands could rehearse, record, and gossip. They called it Courtyard Studios and when local shoe-gazing galacticos Slowdive were produced by Chris Hufford there, the venture took off. Courtyard became Oxford's own Sun Studios.

After Chris Hufford's Damascene conversion at the Jericho, an invitation to Courtyard followed and another On A Friday demo was recorded in October 1991 for £500. The cassette, titled "Manic Hedgehog," after the local record shop that sold it, and with a cover featuring Thom's drawing of an alien and the slogan "work sucks." It included "I Can't," "Thinking About You," and "You," as well as the pedophile's tale "Nothing Touches Me" and the countrified "Phillipa Chicken." Producers Chris Hufford and Bryce Edge's offer to manage them was accepted and the inner circle was complete, until Nigel Godrich engineered *The Bends*.

Predictably, gigs supporting such bands as the mighty Icicle Works and the rather less wondrous Dumpy's Rusty Nuts and Funkin' Barstewards led precisely nowhere. Then the magic happened.

"Creep" felt like a one-hit-wonder's moment in the sun. Almost everyone outside the inner circle felt it.

3
"SEE ALL YOU CREEPS THERE!"

Keith Wozencroft was the Parlophone (an EMI-owned British label) sales representative for the Oxford area. Dark arts often percolated the relations between labels and shops, especially if the shop happened to be a chart return shop (i.e. one of the select few where sales counted towards the charts), but reps needed a sunny personality and a degree in small talk. The truth about Keith Wozencroft's latest visit though, as he revealed to Our Price sales assistant Colin Greenwood, was that the rep was exiting sales. He had been promoted into A&R, where he could sign and then nurture bands. Not one to look a gift horse in the mouth, Colin gave Keith Wozencroft a copy of the Dungeon tape.

He listened. Inexperienced he may have been, but Keith Wozencroft heard something in On A Friday's studio work that had eluded everyone else. Soon he was at an open-air concert at Oxford's South Park to hear them play. Since it was held at the end of October, the weather was brisk and the attendance sparse, but Keith Wozencroft knew his ears had not deceived him, and soon he was presenting the Manic Hedgehog demo to his overlords at EMI. The company turned up en masse at the next Jericho Tavern show in November.

Suddenly, On A Friday were big fish, although the pond remained small. Alongside the EMI contingent, there were over twenty A&R men (they were all men) at the Jericho. Offers flew in, but Keith Wozencroft's boss, former Dexys Midnight Runner Nick Gatfield, promised a certain amount of artistic freedom, always a winner with stroppy new bands, although it will be invariably sacrificed when bands drive into the rough.

In early December, they secured their first magazine cover: Oxford's local hipster bible *Curfew*. They're there in black and white above advertisements for a Mexican restaurant with a giant video screen and a lighting hire company. Thom is wearing shades; the others lurk guiltily behind him, heads tilted at assorted unappealing angles.

On a Friday—December 20, 1991—On A Friday traveled to London, to EMI's offices in Manchester Square, site of The Beatles' iconic cover photographs on *Please Please Me* and the *Red* and *Blue* albums. They signed to Parlophone on a six-album deal. Permanently in debt as a student, Thom's first reaction was to pay off those debts: "The banker came across the desk to shake my hand. I told him to fuck off."

A six-album deal with Parlophone didn't mean Radiohead were guaranteed to make six albums for Parlophone, merely that, after their debut, the record company had five options to allow them to make another. However, On A Friday weren't a tax loss. Following The Sundays and Stephen Duffy, they were the third and final act to sign to the label that year. They wanted to succeed; Parlophone wanted them to succeed; Keith Wozencroft needed them to succeed.

"We wanted to cut through all that 'paying your dues' shit," explained Thom succinctly to *Curfew*. "Everybody slagged us off, but all the indie labels had distribution deals with majors." The song that had really impressed another EMI boss, Rupert Perry, was "Phillipa Chicken." He told them he relished them recording it properly. Jonny told him it was no longer part of their repertoire.

There was one glaring problem: the name. In February, it had already been derided in *Melody Maker* as being "apt for beer-gutted pub rockers, but ill-suited to the astonishing intensity of this bunch," by the otherwise supportive John Harris, who would be instrumental in introducing the band to highly rated, super-hip publicists Hall or Nothing. When Parlophone pressed for change, they were pushing at an open door since On A Friday didn't actually like being On A Friday. In March, Keith Wozencroft suggested a list of potential new names: the long-dumped Gravitate (ugh), Jude (hell's bells), and, possibly the worst of a lamentable bunch, The Music, a name which would be taken by some fleetingly popular indie hopefuls years later.

There was another name, Radiohead. Seductively, it was borrowed from the accordion-led "Radio Head," from band favorites Talking Heads' *True Stories* album and it presciently trilled "radio head, the sound of a brand-new world." The song itself is a sweet, slender thing, but Radiohead? It sounded right. It still does. To celebrate they went on a tour with The Catherine Wheel, a cacophonous, swirling ensemble led by Rob Dickinson, cousin of Bruce Dickinson, singer of EMI's Iron Maiden.

Now there was pressure beyond their failed attempts to spend all their label's parsimonious clothing allowance: Thom spent £30 at Oxfam, but Ed did acquire a lovely white shirt. The era of record labels nurturing acts, REO Speedwagon-style, through a slew of feet-finding albums wasn't quite over, but the window of opportunity before Parlophone lost patience would close fast and Radiohead had to deliver reasonably quickly. Initially, they took comfort in what they knew. They returned to Courtyard, keeping Chris Hufford and Bryce Edge as producers as they resurrected a couple of Manic Hedgehog songs, "You," where a pair of lovers perish, and "Thinking About You," alongside two new songs, the Pixies-lite "Prove Yourself" and, mentally scarred by a road accident he'd had before going to Exeter, Thom's first anti-car polemic, "Stupid Car." They called it the *Drill* EP and it was released on May 5, 1992.

Bizarrely, they secured national daytime airplay. Gary Davies, a silky-smooth Radio 1 DJ whose jingles went "Oooh, Gary Davies; oooh, Gary Davies" and who had no obvious track record of affection for Pixies, light or heavy, loved "Prove Yourself" and made it his Happening Track of the Week. The song was Thom's living in Oxford lament: "this constant feeling nobody wanted me to be there, no-one gave a fuck about me," as he told *NME*. It was a false dawn. For all Parlophone's muscle and Gary Davies's patronage, the muddy sounding *Drill* EP stalled at 101. Years later, one of the band (the DJ couldn't tell them apart) would bump into Gary Davies. The thanks were profuse and genuine.

Chris Hufford and Bryce Edge producing their clients was a far from desirable situation for both parties. The circle needed to be unbroken. On the other side of the Atlantic, the ultra-hip production team of Sean Slade and Paul Q. Kolderie had been making a small name for themselves at their ultra-hip Fort Apache studios in Roxbury, Boston's most ultra-hip suburb, not least in producing ultra-hip Buffalo Tom's titanic *Let Me Come Over* album. When the pair came to Britain on a scouting trip, they were pleased to meet Radiohead at Nick Gatfield's prompting, but since Paul Q. Kolderie had engineered Pixies' *Surfer Rosa* album, not as pleased as Radiohead were to meet them. The Americans were soon aboard.

In September, Radiohead played the EMI conference and the Paul Q. Kolderie and Sean Slade-produced *Creep* EP emerged. It performed better than *Drill*, selling six thousand copies in the UK, and for one week it was the seventy-eighth most popular single in the land. "Creep" itself had potential though, didn't it? EMI thought so; the band thought so; the producers thought so; and the management thought so. Clearly not. Oh well. Silly them. Clairvoyant Thom was undaunted as he told *NME*: "In 10 years, people will be playing 'Creep' and saying it's a fucking classic record. We know that."

Later that month, they went into Chipping Norton Recording Studios, twenty-one miles north-west of Oxford, to record the rest of the album. Although Phil's new Morris Minor gave them new flexibility, and Colin had a biker girlfriend called Madeleine, the recording sessions were brief and unpleasant, but, hey, they would soon become long and unpleasant. "It was," noted Paul Q. Kolderie to Q with admirable understatement, "a bit of a struggle." Aside from "I Can't" and "Lurgee," as originally helmed by Chris Hufford at Courtyard, it was recorded in three weeks. Problems were legion: "We didn't know how to use a studio," admitted Thom to Vox. EMI wanted hits, which always seemed unlikely, and the songs? Hmm. "It's a snapshot of them developing," the roll-ups smoking Chris Hufford told Mojo many years later. "It's a collection of our greatest hits as an unsigned band," quipped Ed, with equal accuracy. By November the ordeal was over, bar the mixing. More trouble.

Paul Q. Kolderie and Sean Slade had tried to fashion a final mix with the band hovering, unsatisfied with everything. With nothing going anywhere, EMI sent the producers, but not the band, back to Fort Apache. There, the pair mixed in peace. The band had no say in the final cut.

With Charlie Myatt at ABS, then ITB and later 13 Artists, as their high-powered agent—he too would last the course—it was tour time and they set off, alongside increasingly suitable acts (if we agree to forget about Doctor and the Medics), such as The Frank and Walters, Machine Gun Feedback, Sultans of Ping FC, James, and Kingmaker.

Throughout the following year, visitors to Thom's kitchen would find his fridge rammed with beer: the riders he'd never drunk, liberated from dressing rooms. The relentless touring served to test themselves outside the Oxford bubble, to hone new material in front of strangers, and to get good, to get really good. The road warriors' reward? A Christmas review in NME, the British music scene's long-term arbiter of cool, describing them as "pitiful, a lily-livered excuse for a rock 'n' roll group."

In February 1993, Radiohead's usual set-opener "Anyone Can Play Guitar" scraped into the British Top 40. For all the knockbacks the band were enduring, it oozed confidence, taking pot-shots at proper pop stars and the deification of sacred cow Jim Morrison in Oliver Stone's biopic without sacrificing its mainstream, almost Merseybeat bent or its fondness for both U2 and Carter the Unstoppable Sex Machine's "Do Re Me So Far So Good." Just to prove the title's mischievous point, anyone who was around the studio at the time, from cooks to secretaries, did play guitar, while Jonny strummed his Fender with a paintbrush: much later, they would claim the song was a celebration of DIY music. Later that month, Radiohead's debut album, *Pablo Honey*, was released in the UK.

Its title came from a tape given to them by yet another local band, Chapterhouse, which included a brief, then-unreleased sketch by platinum-selling New York telephone pranksters The Jerky Boys. In it, a mother asked unsuspecting Pablo if he is "washing your ass, keeping yourself clean." It's funnier to listen to.

Pablo Honey is an unsatisfying collection that pigeonholed Radiohead for the last time. Paul Q. Kolderie and Sean Slade gave them an American sheen, but at its Pixies- and U2-influenced heart it's a major label version of a British indie album. There's indie landfill such as "I Can't" and "Prove Yourself," but even beyond "Creep" and the other standout, the oldest track, "Stop Whispering" (not that the band were happy with the album version), signposts to a better future abounded: the cascading Magazine-esque guitars of "Ripcord"; the manner in which the sneering "How Do You?" veers from by-numbers punk to avant thrash and, in its last seconds, tinkling piano; the almost-jazz beginning (so smooth Al Jarreau could have sung over it) to Jonny's US favorite track, the closer, "Blow Out," before the guitars kicked in. More encouraging still was the gulf in quality between *Pablo Honey*'s sedate, majestic stroll through "Thinking About You" and the squelching *Drill* EP version. This radically reworked version of the masturbation ode become Brenda Greenwood's favorite track by her boys: "Don't tell her what it's about," begged Jonny of *Select*.

Lyrically, Thom was laying down markers. "Lurgee" was a corruption of an eighteenth-century slang term for skiving, resurrected by Spike Milligan in "Lurgi Strikes Britain," a 1954 episode of *The Goon Show*,

PABLO HONEY

RECORDED AT Chipping Norton
Recording Studios and Courtyard
Studios, Oxfordshire

PRODUCED BY Sean Slade, Paul Q.
Kolderie & Chris Hufford

PERSONNEL

Thom E. Yorke: vocals, guitar
Jonny Greenwood: lead guitar,
    piano, organ
Ed O'Brien: guitar, vocals
Colin Greenwood: bass guitar
Phil Selway: drums

COVER ART

Lisa Bunny Jones: paintings
Icon: design
Tom Sheehan: photography

RELEASED Feb 22, 1993

LABEL Parlophone, CDPCS 7360

TRACK LIST

You
Creep
How Do You?
Stop Whispering
Thinking About You
Anyone Can Play Guitar
Ripcord
Vegetable
Prove Yourself
I Can't
Lurgee
Blow Out

"Pablo Honey is an unsatisfying collection which pigeon-holed Radiohead for the last time."

where "lurgi" was an unconvincing bout of influenza. The song of that name was Thom dipping his hurty toe into ailments for the first time, and if there was self-laceration on "I Can't," the uninspired, Parlophone-questioning "Ripcord," and "Thinking About You," where Thom cast himself as a pop star's whiny ex, then the lashing out on "Vegetable" was worthy of Elvis Costello, so venerated by Thom and Jonny that Thom would claim, possibly untruthfully, not to have washed his hands for six months after their meeting.

Ultimately, as most reviews concurred, *Pablo Honey* was flawed but promising, or "promisingly imperfect" as *Melody Maker* adroitly decided, while *NME*'s observation that "it's much less variable than expected," had a similar ring of truth. The Boo Radleys, Slowdive, and PJ Harvey made better albums in 1993, but EMI were distracted by the commercial disaster that was Blur's *Modern Life Is Rubbish*, so, luckily, *Pablo Honey* initially slipped under the British radar.

In other news, Yoav Kutner, Israel's John Peel, a DJ at army radio station Galatz, fell for "Creep" hook, line, and sinker and it reached the top of the country's charts: Radiohead's first No. 1. As Britain shrugged its shoulders at *Pablo Honey*, Radiohead played three spring nights in Tel Aviv to frenzied acclaim, and love affairs were born both between band and country and Jonny and Sharona Katan, aka visual artist Shin Katan, whom he would marry in 1995. Their children (Tamir, born 2002; Omri, born 2005; Zohar, born 2008) would be raised in the Jewish faith. "Me and Jonny are private people," she insisted. "Radiohead aren't my life. I keep things separate. We don't talk about Jonny's work at home."

As formal confirmation of just how underwhelmed everyone outside Israel was, when Radiohead released a new single in May, it didn't come from *Pablo Honey*. A strong candidate for career nadir, "Pop Is Dead" guiltily tiptoed to No. 42 in the British charts. Brief, dull, and described by Ed as "a hideous mistake," the Americans refused to release it at all. It sniped at more successful peers, and if Thom had been coy at naming names in song, once he had anointed Jim Morrison as "a bimbo," he was more than willing to expand to *NME*. "Am I really supposed to be excited or even challenged by Suede? There's more art in Pot Noodle or Tango advertisements." He had a point, but Suede were having hits.

What now? There was only one solution and it involved building their audience in the most traditional way. Over the next two years—albeit in evolving circumstances—they would play over 350 gigs.

Magic had been in short supply since Keith Wozencroft's fateful visit to Oxford Our Price. "Pop Is Dead" suggested they were out of magic. There's always magic left though. The game was about to change once more.

By the time *Pablo Honey* was released, "Creep" had been and gone in the UK, just another flop single, but the Israelis weren't the only ones who'd fallen for its charms. The Norwegians were very taken and so were the Spanish and the New Zealanders. Slim pickings, but more places to play.

"Creep" was conceived by Thom in Exeter while he was mulling over his past infatuation with his dismissively acid-tongued amour in Oxford. To this day he maintains she knows who she is, but sensibly, she has kept her own counsel. It sounded so much like The Hollies' 1974 global hit "The Air That I Breathe" that its creators, Albert Hammond and Mike Hazlewood, would eventually be given songwriting credits. Paul Q. Kolderie and Sean Slade misheard one of Thom's studio mumbles and thought it was a Scott Walker song rather than a Scott Walker influenced song. First impressions were muted: Keith Wozencroft had initially thought it wasn't a single and Jonny reckoned it was too wimpy in its initial acoustic state.

When Jonny suggested some fierce guitar might exacerbate Thom's self-loathing, he was attempting to undermine a song he had no time for. Jonny's guitar fury gave this description of an imperious woman and her wretched, wraith-like suitor new life and everything bar piano and some vocal overdubs was recorded in one take. Jonny then decided it was something special, so very special. Not always one to shoot himself in the foot, Thom recorded an airplay-friendly version, replacing the word "fucking" with the word "very." Not that it mattered when Britain's Radio 1 decided "Creep" was too depressing to be inflicted on the general public, but Thom's willingness to play ball would soon prove to be an airplay-generating masterstroke.

Then, unaware of its minor success elsewhere, Aaron Axelsen, a DJ at KCRH, a tiny East Bay radio station, began to play the album track "Creep." Axelson also worked for KITS (Live 105), an influential alternative rock station in San Francisco. It too began to play "Creep." People asked to hear it again. The more influential still KROQ-FM, another station owned by the same company, began to play it in Los Angeles. Again, listeners were keen. Suddenly, Radiohead had traction and national airplay. At the turn of the year, Capitol (their US label, which, like Parlophone, was part of EMI) released it as a single. Slowly but surely, "Creep"—rather than the band who made it—began to conquer the United States, and when the band arrived at Capitol's Los Angeles office in May, the hitherto uninterested staff were wearing Radiohead T-shirts. All of them. "The doors opened before we were really ready," admitted Thom.

There were myriad benefits. Now, the Americans got behind *Pablo Honey* and there was no danger of Radiohead being dropped or downgraded. "Creep" meant EMI picked up their option for album number two, the last time this would be an issue. This second benison was rather murkier: "priority" acts gobbled up a label's time, manpower, and resources. "Creep" meant, in Parlophone terms, the difference between Radiohead being Bliss and being Pet Shop Boys. Radiohead were now a priority act and the American rise of "Creep" meant *Pablo Honey* was rediscovered across the world. The gigs were slightly bigger, the press keener and the ennui seemingly dispersed.

All was not quite as it seemed. Then and now, "Creep" was unrepresentative of Radiohead and of *Pablo Honey*. There was something else. The success of "Creep" felt like a one-hit-wonder's moment in the sun. It was even, whisper it soft, a novelty record. Almost everyone outside the inner circle felt it, and they felt it more acutely when it was clear there was no "Creep II" in the locker.

And, let's remember who we were dealing with. Radiohead had made compromises. They'd cut out the dues-paying, but fame affects everyone in different ways, few of which are positive. The crux is that no musician is truly prepared for fame's downsides: for the little humiliations, the sheer drudgery, the temptations, the early mornings, the frustrations, and the way the music gets put on the back burner. Radiohead had become the "Creep" guys and they struggled. This wasn't what it was about for them, and they soon rued spurning Blur's generous offer of a mutual drink and an explanation of just what slogging across the United States entailed.

After their first American date (June 22, 1993, at Boston's Venus de Milo: "See all you Creeps there!" trilled the flyer), few of those about 350 "Creep"-spawned shows were enjoyable, even the ones with musical soulmates Belly in September, although as Colin fondly remembered, "We would park in the center of the town, trawl the book and record shops and enjoy meeting local people." Nobody regretted spurning an opportunity to support labelmates Duran Duran in American arenas. The Australian dates were soul-destroying, but a one-off, post-Belly date supporting Tears For Fears at Las Vegas's Aladdin Theatre, for which they had flown across the US, was worse still. The Tears For Fears crew treated them like serfs and as revenge Thom kicked in some of their lighting. Keen students of irony may wish to note that Tears For Fears then began to cover "Creep."

The band members slipped into clearly defined roles. Having a mutual interest in cigarettes and the country soul of Dan Penn, Colin—who had wanted US success more than the rest and more than success at home—and sleeptalking Ed shared a room. Increasingly introverted, Jonny listened to Sherlock Holmes audiobooks. Phil, so placid they nicknamed him Mad Dog ("He's very cerebral, very thoughtful," noted Ed, "not one to go smashing TV sets through windows."), devoured his favorite meal of steak and potatoes, shrugged when he was mistaken for the bus driver, and spent endless hours on the phone arranging his forthcoming wedding. When he wasn't traveling to shows by car so he could read, Thom wrote new songs on his guitar. When laryngitis forced him to ask Rachel Owen to telephone management and cancel the band's prestigious Reading Festival slot on the day ("I couldn't speak, let alone sing.") and Eat were forced to deputize, the perception was that Radiohead were, well, a lily-livered excuse for a pop group after all.

Thom wasn't bearing up at all well. "I got angry," he told the BBC in 2019. "I got more control freakish, I became more unbearable. I put my hands on the steering wheel and white knuckled. I didn't care who I hurt until the end of *OK Computer*. Years later, I apologized to the guys." Whatever he imagined success to be like, it wasn't this, and until he swapped his dark basement flat for the three-bedroomed, detached "House That 'Creep' Built" in the Oxford suburb of Headington (mortgage not cash) the day before the Belly dates, his only other extravagance had been a Sony Walkman and that fleeting moment when he had gold discs on his walls: "It made me feel like a rock star, briefly."

By this time, they had established their financial template. All five members would share the proceeds of everything, except for songwriting, which, explained Thom, "We divide according to who wrote what. We don't argue about it, but it takes ages."

Domesticity would never be Thom's forte and when Rachel Owen went away for a few winter days, their oriental fish died because he was incapable of rousing himself to break a hole in the ice. He fantasized about a solo career. "I thought I could go it alone," he told *NME*. "I thought I didn't need anybody. But I fucking do."

By the time of the Belly dates, *Pablo Honey* had gone gold in the United States and *Rolling Stone* had anointed "Creep" as "the most audacious pop move since 'Every Breath You Take.'" Reissued in the UK, "Creep" reached No. 7, but every victory was Pyrrhic. They briefly repositioned themselves as tea-drinking British fops who covered the very American "Rhinestone Cowboy." The affectation wasn't wholly fake. Ed claimed to have spurned a lady's offer of cocaine and, it seems fair to assume, sex, in her hotel room in Dallas ("I was just flabbergasted," he spluttered, far from convincingly), and Thom tried to explain to *Vox* that the foppishness was a joke: "I love getting stoned, but I don't go on chat shows and talk about it because it's purely recreational and I go through phases of drinking myself into the ground." He claimed much of *Pablo Honey* was recorded under the influence of cannabis, but few believed him.

Unusually for a band who ambled onstage to the sound of the cello and piano of Olivier Messiaen's *Quartet for the End of Time*, a piece written in the Silesian prison camp to which the Nazis had sent him, Radiohead were forced to endure the ignominy of playing "Creep" and "Anyone Can Play Guitar" at an MTV Beach House Party as barely dressed models-actresses-whatevers gyrated around them. It was a sunny day, turning cloudy only when Radiohead played. Thom had to be rescued when he dived in and his heavy boots filled with water.

They recorded a jingle for KROQ saying the station's programs were "so fucking special" and guested on its *Loveline* show, although nobody had told them it was a cesspit of dysfunctional darkness which needed a psychiatrist in attendance rather than a pop group. When an out-of-his-depth Ed claimed he would sleep with a fourteen-year-old girl if she was mature enough, the worst of times became worse still.

Thom decided blond hair extensions were the way forward, and there was a fashion shoot for Iceberg jeans which would never be spoken of again. Little wonder that when they sent a copy of *Pablo Honey* to John Leckie, producer of Magazine's *Real Life* ("One of the greatest records ever made," gushed Thom) and eighties XTC spin-offs The Dukes of Stratosphear, with a view to future collaboration, he wasn't interested, claiming it was "too noisy." "It could be worse," shrugged Thom to *Vox*, "I could be a Mod."

Before "Stop Whispering," the American follow-up to "Creep" and another reminder that there was nothing akin to the hit in the locker, flopped, there were European dates with James, which were a delight. The shows would go well, but the band's alcohol consumption had sky-rocketed and when the carnival began in Hamburg on November 11, there was a band meeting. Views were aired, drink was drunk, fingers were pointed, "Creep" was derided and the prospect of divorce loomed. Were they happy? No. Had they handled success well? No. Could they carry on like this? Absolutely not.

There was hope if they chose to embrace it. "Creep" had given them some short-term clout, and the new songs Thom had been strumming were taking loose shape. What if, from now on, they did things their way? There were five answers: yes, yes, yes, yes, and yes.

At the 1994 BRIT Awards, which honored music that had made an impact in 1993, "Creep" was second only to Take That's "Pray" in the British Single of the Year category. Radiohead would never be quite so mainstream again.

"I got angry. I got more control freakish, I became more unbearable. I put my hands on the steering wheel and white knuckled." THOM

"The Benz" became "The Bends" and everything began to change.

4
COMING UP FOR AIR

1994 would be the year Radiohead took control. Playing only one date until a European tour in May, they began it rehearsing the twenty-four songs Thom had developed on the tour bus in The Barn That "Creep" Built: Canned Applause, a converted, soundproofed apple shed on an Oxfordshire fruit farm, initially with no toilets and no running water, but with a lovely view of Didcot Power Station. Chris Hufford and Bryce Edge wouldn't be producing Radiohead again, ensuring the relationship would continue. Paul Q. Kolderie and Sean Slade still had the backing of Capitol, but the band and Parlophone were less sure.

Renewed attempts were made to entice John Leckie. Having been tape operator for George Harrison and Phil Spector on *All Things Must Pass*, and engineer on Syd Barrett's last sessions, Leckie was no malleable pawn, but he was battered and bruised from attempting to make some of the second Stone Roses album listenable. Radiohead rustled up a selection of the new material and sent him a tape. The first outsider to note the first great leap forward, this time Leckie was interested, once he'd finished producing Ride's career-halting *Carnival of Light*.

With the second album scheduled for October 1994, on February 21, Radiohead and Leckie decamped to RAK, where Nigel Godrich, whom Leckie had mentored, was house engineer. The lavishly appointed studio was a stone's throw from Regent's Park in London and owned by producer Mickie Most when it was the RAK label's (part of EMI of course) hit factory as Suzi Quatro, Mud, Smokie, and a host of others bashed out a succession of Most-produced hits seemingly every week in the 1970s. Radiohead plumped for Studio 1, the one with the most natural light.

Things would get better, but first they had to get much worse. Band and label were on different roads. Understandably in the wake of "Creep," Parlophone wanted hits; Radiohead wanted to exorcise the ghosts of "Creep" in their own way. Result: paralysis. Not for the last time, like the lotharios they weren't, Radiohead could not commit. Even the unflappable Leckie was flapping, but his hands-off serenity, his willingness to allow them to do *The Guardian*'s crossword in worktime and to consume chemical relaxants would be crucial in the months to come. "We were scared of our instruments," lamented Thom to *Vox*. "There wasn't enough energy."

Ed thought they were over-questioning everything, but the real problem wasn't merely the label's demands for hits, it was their demand that they heard the hits first. "It set the album off on the wrong track," Jonny told *Select*. "The first two months were a total fucking meltdown." Every few days a different record company man would happen to be passing RAK and would drop in to hear some hits. They'd hear a drum track if they were lucky.

Radiohead had "The Bends" (or "The Benz" as it was initially known), "Sulk," and "(Nice Dream)," magnificent songs which would be the bedrock of the rebirth, but hardly radio-friendly unit shifters and, in the US, Capitol became increasingly reluctant to formally green light. In the end, the second single would be a demo of the elderly "High and Dry" but right now Radiohead were cranking up Thom's vocals and Jonny's guitars until everything, except sales potential, was too big. In hindsight, this soul-crushing period would be referred to as the "November Rain" months. "It was," noted the laconic Leckie, "a bit much to take." Even the management lost faith, taking the insurance policy of signing another Oxford band, Supergrass. They secured them a major deal. With Parlophone of course.

THE BENDS

RECORDED AT RAK and Abbey Road, London; The Manor, Oxfordshire

PRODUCED BY John Leckie

PERSONNEL
Thom Yorke: lead vocals, guitars, piano; string arrangements
Jonny Greenwood: guitar, organ, recorder, synthesizer, piano; string arrangements
Ed O'Brien: guitar, backing vocals
Colin Greenwood: bass
Phil Selway: drums

COVER ART
Stanley Donwood: fine art
The White Chocolate Farm: fine art
Green Ink: painting

RELEASED Mar 13, 1995

LABEL Parlophone, CDPCS 7372

HIGHEST CHART POSITION ON RELEASE UK 4, US 88, AUS 23, SWE 26, GER 73, NZ 8, CAN 14, NL 20

TRACK LIST
Planet Telex
The Bends
High & Dry
Fake Plastic Trees
Bones
(Nice Dream)
Just
My Iron Lung
Bullet Proof . . . I Wish I Was
Black Star
Sulk
Street Spirit (Fade Out)

"We wanted it to sound a bit sinister." JOHN LECKIE

Beyond teaching Radiohead how to record guitars, Leckie's master-stroke was to temporarily dump Ed, Colin, Phil, and Jonny in order to allow Thom to work things through with an acoustic guitar and a drum machine. When the foursome returned, Thom had nailed "Fake Plastic Trees" and the clouds began to disperse.

After nine weeks' recording with only Sundays off, in May and June they road-tested the new material in Europe and then Australasia, dis-covering what worked and what didn't, what to keep and what to jettison, and by the time the European leg finished at London's Astoria on May 27, 1994, they were sizzling. MTV recorded the show, which became the *Live at the Astoria* video, and when, a little later, it was time to record "My Iron Lung," it was decided that the backing track from the Astoria was untop-pable and it made *The Bends*, almost undoctored.

With the band revitalized by the tour, Leckie subtly changed their environment and they moved to the Manor Studio, north of Oxford. Here they would master rather than be mastered by the technology. Then, fueled by copious amounts of cannabis (they claimed), the dam burst and almost everything was completed in a spurt of creativity. "We wanted to get in the right frame of mind and we had. Eventually," noted Thom. In August, Leckie mixed "My Iron Lung" and a slew of B-sides at Abbey Road, but first there was a Glastonbury appearance and a cathar-tic, demons-banishing Reading Festival date. There was another jaunt around the UK, and dates in Bangkok and in Mexico, where there was a band meeting even more frank than the one in Hamburg: "Years and years of tension and not saying anything to each other came out," Thom told *NME*. Shows in the United States had been booked for October and November to coincide with the album's release, but for all the studio toil, that deadline was out of the question.

It wasn't all sweetness and light: at a cramped but memorably marvel-ous gig in Guadalajara, Mexico, Phil played the show surrounded by local heavyweights about whom he thought wise not to complain, while a solitary and out-of-sorts Ed, unplacated by the acquisition of The Cottage That "Creep" Built (his mother's first present for her boy's new abode was a fish steamer, but the ceilings were so low he developed a stoop), overturned a table in a Los Angeles restaurant on the last date. Back home, they recorded "Sulk" at Abbey Road over a relaxed weekend during which they would also exhume the "High & Dry" demo, forget their fears that it would be their "Mull of Kintyre," and hoist it onto the album.

Thom had written the first half of "My Iron Lung" on the morning he'd cancelled Reading '93 and the remainder on the tour bus. Lyrically, it was a direct kiss-off to "Creep," "the final nail in the coffin of a song which shall remain nameless," said Thom, far from cryptically. Another example of his medical fixation, it took its title from the photograph of a poorly fifties child encased in an iron lung which Thom claimed to have carried with him at Exeter and had rather neglectfully lost. It wasn't "Creep," then, but it was a gentle evolution from *Pablo Honey* and the middle eight marked Jonny's first dalliance with strings. The radical departure would come with much of the rest of *The Bends*. Radio 1 wouldn't play the single—too raucous apparently—but the newly burgeoning Radiohead fan base took it to 24 in the British charts.

That and the single's sales of twenty thousand wasn't nearly enough for EMI, who, having finally come to terms with the fact that there would never be a "Creep II," remained troubled by the lack of obvious hits. When John Leckie came to mix the whole album, he discovered that the label had re-recruited Paul Q. Kolderie and Sean Slade to mix all bar three tracks, in order to provide the American sheen which had probably done *Pablo Honey* no harm.

With the album in the bag, Phil married Caitlin Morrison and honeymooned in the not especially rock 'n' roll Lyme Regis, a sleepy coastal town in south-west England best known for its harbor wall, The Cobb, as featured in the film version of local resident John Fowles's novel *The French Lieutenant's Woman*. Jonny and Thom played some American acoustic shows, and the whole band played a pre-Christmas knees up at the Jericho Tavern, billed as Faithless and the Wonder Boys (the B-side to "Anyone Can Play Guitar"). There's light at the end of even the darkest tunnel: the American producers accepted there was little work to be done; more reluctantly, Leckie accepted two pairs of fresh ears wouldn't hurt and *The Bends* was finished at Fort Apache.

Having eased themselves from the pigeonholes of being an indiepop band on a major label, shoegazers, and a novelty act, something else loomed in 1995: Britpop. It barely registered in the United States, but in Britain the battle between semi-feral Mancunians Oasis and the faux Cockney geezers of Blur reached the BBC's flagship *Nine O'Clock News*. Thom cannily stayed clear: "The British music scene is so insular, so petty and so bitchy I don't want any contact with it." As with every musical movement, there were many more losers than winners and "My Iron Lung" placed Radiohead in danger of getting sucked into the vortex as Britpop also-rans. In Los Angeles, Capitol began to have new doubts. Nobody was wearing Radiohead T-shirts anymore.

Released on February 27, 1995, a fortnight before the release of its parent album in the UK, their defiantly non-Britpop "High & Dry" marked the beginning of the turnaround. It took them into the British Top 20 again. More significantly still, it was their first US hit since "Creep," a No. 78 hit, but a hit all the same.

The song itself was the oldest on *The Bends*. Indeed, it went all the way back to Thom's Exeter days with Headless Chicken when it was a galloping punk song about "some loony girl I was going out with," he told *Billboard*. The Radiohead demo version they had considered for *Pablo Honey* was based around a Soul II Soul sample. They returned to it while casting around for *Bends* material. Phil had acquired new drums and he wanted to take them for a safety lap; Thom sang like interesting-era Rod Stewart, but it was dumped again. Third time around, they resurrected it at RAK, fell in love with the Rod Stewart demo all over again, and put that version on the album, almost untouched. Thom wore a Charles Bukowski T-shirt when they played it on *Top of the Pops* and, in a bravura display of self-confidence, he sported a badge declaring "I Am A Creep" on the video made for the British market.

Six months late, *The Bends* finally surfaced on March 13, 1995 in the UK and three weeks later in the US, where the album would reach No. 88 as opposed to *Pablo Honey*'s 32: it would sell more copies over the long haul. Not for the last time, the change from album to album was seismic. It took its title from the colloquial name given to DCS (decompression sickness), from which divers suffer when rising too quickly. As Lieutenant Axel explains in Jennifer Egan's *Manhattan Beach* novel: "The nitrogen bubbles trapped in the blood must find a way out, so they push through the soft tissues. Men bleed from their eyes, nose and ears." The pain is acute and hard to shake, a little like Radiohead's "Creep" experience. And there's that word "bends": Radiohead's world is full of them.

After a successful collaboration on the single "My Iron Lung," the sleeve would become the first Radiohead album to feature the work of Thom's visual arts collaborator, Dan Rickwood (aka Stanley Donwood), a friend from Exeter, who noted that "Thom is mouthy and pissed off. Someone I could work with." It showed a resuscitation dummy used at Oxford's John Radcliffe Hospital blended with Thom's face, given an expression poised somewhere between agony and orgasmic ecstasy, just like the contents. Inside there were apparently photos of a Japanese car salesman, of the belly of a Gulf War soldier, and of New Zealand pedestrians, but they were so distorted they could have been anything. To complete the picture, Thom scribbled random thoughts about bank clerks and "the soft warm radiance of money."

Musically, Phil, Colin, Jonny, and Ed were contributing more than on *Pablo Honey*, and that things round here were different was clear from the very first, wobbly, cut-up seconds of the opening "Planet Telex," which handily suggested a diver coming up for air as much as a new musical direction. By the closing "Street Spirit (Fade Out)," it was far from clear whether Thom's departing benediction to "immerse your soul in love" was balm or obituary.

Of course, "My Iron lung" and "High & Dry" were familiar and the fan base were no strangers to the road-tested "(Nice Dream)," "The Bends," and, by the end of 1994, "Bones," "Black Star," "Street Spirit (Fade Out)," and "Fake Plastic Trees." Even so, this was a new Radiohead and even the jokes were different: where *Pablo Honey* took its name from childish pranksters, *The Bends* was dedicated to Bill Hicks, the recently deceased comedian of an altogether darker hue: "I smoke to fill the potholes in my soul." They were now fiendishly difficult to categorize, but they certainly weren't Britpop, and when their foes at *NME* pronounced *The Bends* Indie Album of the Year, Radiohead reprinted the quote as a sales aid, leaving out the word "indie," a stunt which made the band chuckle more than Howard Stern's New York radio station WXRK, which handed out condoms at Radiohead concerts. One side of the wrap featured *The Bends* artwork; the other declared "Our Listeners Come First."

This wasn't a concept album, but there was a lyrical thrust with Thom delving deeper into his recurring themes of dislocation, rebirth, and technology troubles. For ones keen to escape "Creep," an awful lot of it was actually about "Creep" and the effect of the song's slow-drip success, not unlike how Nirvana's *In Utero* had kicked back against "Smells Like Teen Spirit." "It's cynical and nervous," admitted Thom, who had a brief but intense love affair with John Lennon's primal-scream fueled *Plastic Ono Band* album which Leckie had worked on, and a more durable relationship with Tom Waits's *The Asylum Years* compilation.

"There's the feeling that something is wrong, but you can't work out what it is."

Its charms remain undiluted all these years later. "Planet Telex," formerly "Planet Xerox" until the titular organization claimed copyright, was the only *The Bends* song written in the studio, although its drum loop was recycled from the ever-resurfacing B-side "Killer Cars." Its opening line, "You can force it, but it will not come," suggested a difficult birth, but it was overflowing with ideas: the reverb; the Can of the Krautrockers' extraordinary 1971 album, *Tago Mago* (immersion in Can's entire catalog is akin to a Radiohead road map, although by 2003, even Thom was admitting, "I should have got it out of my system at art college."); "Live and Let Die"; and Thom's hook-laden piano. There was a recording twist beyond engineer Nigel Godrich using an early Apple Mac to edit the drums before returning them to the multitrack. One night, RAK's chef was away, so the band were given money to spend on food. Like the naughty schoolboys they sometimes are, they spent it on drink. When Thom returned, he was far from sober and, disappointingly, his legs had stopped working. He did his vocals in one take at 4am, lying on the studio floor, bottle of wine in hand. That it's so hard to tell is a tribute of sorts.

"The Bends" itself was a cathartic howl, for all Thom's later disclaimer that it was "completely jokey, completely taking the piss and none of it even happened to us; the stuff about an aeroplane was our Bowie pastiche." It was conceived in Phoenix, Arizona, where Thom heard a marching band of eight-year-olds rehearsing, and it was recorded in a rush because Phil had an appointment with a realtor, but this was Jonny's moment. He'd been sterling before, but now he was stellar and the cult of his guitar began here. He genuinely doesn't seem to care, as he told *The Guardian* in 2018: "I'm more proud of what we've written than how I play."

If "The Bends" was the moment when Jonny emerged as a guitarist, "Fake Plastic Trees" was the first lyric Thom was truly satisfied with, hinting at Los Angeles fakery, plastic surgery fakery, and sexual fakery, without ever truly revealing itself. On September 1, the band went to see a Jeff Buckley solo show at London's Garage. Thom came back inspired, tried two unsatisfactory takes and promptly burst into tears, the opening salvo of a lengthy near-tantrum. Again, John Leckie sent four of Radiohead to bed. He gave Thom an acoustic guitar and told the singer to do a guide vocal. Naturally, it was the one which was used.

For extra grandeur, Jonny scored some Samuel Barber-style strings the night before Peter Gabriel collaborator Caroline Lavell added cello and erstwhile Headless Chicken John Matthias viola and violin. The pair became the first outsiders to contribute to a Radiohead song, unless the "Anyone Can Play Guitar" choir counts. As a single it made the British Top 20, but when Capitol recruited the lauded Bob Clearmountain to remix, he removed the strings and keyboards. The band nixed it. "The ghost-like keyboard sounds and weird strings were gutted, like he'd gone in with a razor blade and chopped it all up. It was horrible," muttered Thom to *Vox*.

Thom's medical obsession resurfaced on "Bones," with hints of mental collapse as a side order. Jonny's work was as jagged as Magazine's John McGeogh or one of Mark E. Smith's better Fall guitarists, but a climactic, no-holds-barred guitar squall was swiftly jettisoned.

Vaguely influenced by Kurt Vonnegut's 1963 science fiction novel *Cat's Cradle*, there's a beautiful, almost spiritual undertow to "(Nice Dream)." Dating from 1992 and among the first tracks recorded for *The Bends*, the group were still so unsure of what do with it that a different version would appear on issue thirteen of the short-lived but lovingly assembled CD/magazine *Volume*. The light jazzy strum that breezes across the introduction is reminiscent of Antônio Carlos Jobim, before the song oozes into massed ranks of acoustic guitars, until it explodes and utilizes some Arctic noises which John Leckie apparently sourced from

Vancouver Aquarium. "We wanted it to sound a bit sinister," explained John Leckie. Its lyric concerns connections inspired by a "half-drunk dream," and it peaked with sweet choral backing and Jonny seemingly threatening to burst into Alvin Stardust's "My Coo Ca Choo."

Speaking of John McGeogh, the guitarist's influence was more overt still on "Just," the first song finished at RAK, where a riff almost identical to Magazine's "Shot by Both Sides" underpinned a tale that once again evoked Kurt Cobain's struggles. Thom heard Jonny's blitzkrieg solo which brings the song to its close and declared, "It's the most exciting thing I've ever heard him come up with." He had a point, but others thought it was too close to Suede.

"Just" was the fourth *Bends* single and its video heralded Radiohead's more oblique visual phase. Conceived by director Jamie Thraves, it features an out-of-sorts, suited man, played by Dorian Lough, who lies down on the sidewalk and, via the magic of subtitles, refuses offers of help and understanding. The Good Samaritans become increasingly agitated. The man agrees to reveal what the problem is, "but God forgive me, and God help us all," he tells them, and the crowd lies down with him. What does he say? Nobody knows, since the subtitles stop and the angles make lipreading impossible. Assuming it's not gibberish, those who do know have kept the secret.

The successful tell you success isn't all it's cracked up to be. Perhaps they're just being gatekeepers, but the mostly acoustic "Bullet Proof . . . I Wish I Was" sees Thom yearning for the anonymity he would never again enjoy and, tellingly, it was his track of choice on *The Bends*. "It's like a lot of trains going past," he told *Vox* of a song which was bathed in a patina of drizzly ambience. Recorded on a summer Sunday afternoon, it's the tale of a man begging for armor to safeguard against the slings and arrows of those who would tear him "limb by limb and tooth by tooth." Thom, Colin, and Phil recorded the backing track and left it for

Ed—using his cigarette lighter as a slide—and Jonny to add all sorts of mostly hushed guitar wonder.

When Dad's away, kids will play, and when John Leckie took the day off to attend a wedding, band and engineer Nigel Godrich played very well together when they crafted "Black Star." In truth, it's nobody's idea of a *Bends* peak, but Thom was particularly supportive of Jonny's guitar, while his vocals carried a twinkly melody with an awful lot of glee for one picking over the bones of a moribund suburban relationship. Its quiet-loud-quiet structure made it the closest *The Bends* came to a "Creep" reprise.

"Sulk" began with the sort of scratching The Cure had deployed on "The Caterpillar," before evolving into something that, but for Jonny's chiming guitars, might have been better suited to B-side status. Thom had written a first draft before he left for Exeter after being shaken by the Hungerford massacre of 1987, where unemployed Michael Ryan shot dead sixteen people and himself. But in the wake of Cobain's suicide, Thom changed the line "just shoot your gun" to "you'll never change." What had started out as a likely single soon lost favor and it was the final *The Bends* song to be completed. It had a certain swing and the tambourine was a nice touch, but the fact that it hasn't been played since November 1995 suggests that for all that swing, "Sulk" was a less than great track on a great album.

Although nobody outside the inner circle knew it at the time, Jonny's favourite *The Bends* track, "Street Spirit (Fade Out)," was the first peep into Radiohead's future. That the fifth *Bends* single in the UK reached No. 5, two places above "Creep," was evidence of both *The Bends*'s slow-burning durability and that the fan base would go to new places with their band. With Ed at his most lambent, it's a lavishly layered epic which stays just the right side of pompous, and its black-and-white video varied its film speeds. Inspired by Thom discovering some dead baby sparrows and their eggshells, it was partly a dipping of toes into political waters, albeit indirectly (and, embarrassingly for such literate souls, there was an incorrectly deployed apostrophe on the lyric sheet), part Thom pointing out he was under a lot of strain. It took many plays to sink in, but when it did, it was there for the long haul, although later Thom admitted it was "the dark tunnel without the light at the end" and would confess it was both "completely influenced" by Ben Okri's novel *The Famished Road* and an R.E.M. rip-off. In 2012, The Darkness's version added a new, gloriously daft, layer of hysteria.

"*The Bends* is a real medical album to me," mused Jonny. "All Thom's stuff is about drip-feeds and life-support machines." This time around, the reviews were almost universally positive. The indie ghetto was left behind forever and "Creep" had been relegated to the status of a fairly beloved moment they could resurrect whenever they fancied. Wired ravers were using *The Bends* as a comedown when Robert Miles's "Children" wasn't offering quite enough, but Thom tried to downplay the album's intensity: "Oh for Christ's sake," he told *Melody Maker*'s Caitlin Moran. "I did not write this album for people to slash their fucking wrists to. It isn't my confessional." Later though, he would confide to *Option* magazine that "*The Bends* was an incredibly personal album, which is why I spent most of my time denying it was personal at all."

Ed's take explains Thom's take: "*The Bends* was personal because we were so insecure. We thought we didn't like each other, which was pathetically middle-class and born of people not speaking their minds."

There was a general understanding that Radiohead were genuine contenders. In *The Times*, David Sinclair anointed it the album of the decade, while *Q* declared it "frighteningly good." Not that Thom was impressed: "It wasn't that good," he insisted, far from fairly. Ed was more reasonable: "*The Bends* utterly changed my life." Phil took a different line: "*The Bends* was *Star Wars*: lots of explosions but not much plot. *OK Computer* was *The*

Empire Strikes Back: more ambitious, more complex, more loose ends, but ultimately much better."

The Bends utterly changed the collective's life, too. From now on, having bought their own equipment, they would mostly eschew the £1,000-a-day studio setting, in favor of the independent setup they were beginning to crave. "Technology is part of the creative process and it should be in our hands," argued Thom.

Colin thought *The Bends* was an antidote to the Blur/Oasis rivalry which had sucked the life out of British music in 1995, but he also understood it was a word-of-mouth phenomenon, and although Phil drove home after dates where possible, the British tour saw audience appreciation reach whole new levels. Parlophone did their job, too: each of those five singles revealed a different facet of the parent album and they utilized expensive but effective television promotion. Ten months after its release, *The Bends* reached No. 4 in the UK and was on its way into 1.5 million American homes.

Having used touring as a break during recording, Radiohead did what they were supposed to do and wheeled themselves out once more, sometimes using Laurie Anderson's "O Superman" as their opening music. The schedule was punishing, even by Radiohead standards.

They finished their American tour on July 25 at Northampton, Massachusetts. Suddenly, they were about to get a famous friend. Entranced by the video to "Fake Plastic Trees," R.E.M. leader Michael Stipe purchased *The Bends* and loved it. He invited Radiohead onto R.E.M.'s European and US tour in support of their much-derided *Monster* album. "Shit, shit, shit," said fanboy Thom to Q. "This is R.E.M. and they really like us. No, I mean they really like us. They're not simply being nice." Three days after Northampton (US), the band were supporting R.E.M. at Milton Keynes Bowl, a few miles from Northampton (UK), in front of sixty thousand people.

Having declared that "Radiohead are so good it scares me," Michael Stipe was the guardian angel Thom didn't realize he was looking for, even when he was admitting: "I can't sit still, I play with my Macintosh all day long." Thom adored indie-era R.E.M. and he admired the way Michael Stipe behaved when stardom beckoned: never spurning it, but never becoming one of them, whoever "them" were. And Stipe? He was a fan who saw something of himself in how Thom was behaving.

As the tour rumbled through early August and the bulk of September, Thom and Michael Stipe were invariably huddled together backstage discussing how to save the world, or, more likely, gossiping about nothing like a pair of sixty-somethings over a metaphorical garden fence after Radiohead's thirty-minute set. Inter-band pranks abounded and Thom learned how to be okay with being a star and the first among equals. "We're like the UN," he told *Select*. "The others can veto, but I'm America." They were lessons he'd need to periodically relearn, but like the best guardian angels, Michael Stipe would always be there for him.

Road fatigue ought to have set in: Colin continued to travel with the road crew, fighting off the hangovers by reading Correlli Barnett's *The Collapse of British Power*, which explained why Britain lost its role in the world between 1918 and 1945; Jonny developed some kind of RSI which meant he had to wear an arm-brace, while headphones staunched the bleeding from his ears and *The Sayings of the Vikings*, a book given to him by EMI Norway, soothed his soul. On their days off, Radiohead would breakfast on their customary juice and cereal, hunt down some Marmite for their toast, and, perhaps, check on the high interest deposit accounts in which they preferred to invest.

On September 4, four days before rejoining R.E.M. for the American leg of the tour, they accepted Brian Eno's invitation to contribute to *The Help Album*, a compilation for the War Child charity which featured

Paul McCartney, Paul Weller, Thom's erstwhile punchbag Suede, plus both Oasis and Blur: it raised over £1 million. The inspired gimmick was that each act would record a song in five hours on the same day and the album would be released five days later. Bidding farewell to their comfort zone, Radiohead grappled with "Lucky," a song they had been playing live since July. "There was no thought process," Thom told *Addicted to Noise*. "It just happened without conscious effort." Allegedly an attempt at a happy song, "Lucky" merged a certain penchant for seventies rock with a certain penchant for technology. It hung together rather well, but Radio 1 declared it too harsh and as a single it only reached No. 51: "I'm waiting for the karma police to come and sort it out," quipped Thom, but he was devastated. If keeping that version and using it on the next album (and they did) was a sign of band contentment (and it was), then this was probably the most productive five hours of Radiohead's career. "It was," noted Brian Eno, "the most beautiful song I've heard for a long, long time."

It wasn't all easy productivity and more high jinks with R.E.M. A Vancouver date for the Canadian industry ended in tears with Thom branding the chattering guests "the rudest fuckers we've ever met" and, the more Canadian press he did, the more Jonny wanted to sign to an indie label and take things down a notch or two. He battled boredom by attempting to say "bollocks" and "wanker" in every radio interview.

Dates with Soul Asylum, hardly musical soulmates but splendid road companions, came to a grim head in Denver in October, when Radiohead's equipment was stolen, forcing Thom and Jonny to play one of their acoustic sets. Yet another headlining tour of Europe followed, but Thom wasn't at his perkiest, driving to gigs with Jonny and management and deciding that the excess fluid in his ear meant he was going deaf like some of his ancestors. He started wearing earplugs, but when he collapsed in Munich in November, drawing some of his own blood, *NME* decided he'd had a rock-star-style tantrum. He was furious and the long-standing feud was reignited.

Only the *Smash Hits* Pollwinners Party in early December alongside the pop poppets of Take That, East 17, and Boyzone offered light relief. "We did 'My Iron Lung' of all things," chuckled Ed to *Melody Maker*. "We stood by the stage for half an hour and it was bedlam: all these girls just screaming and shouting. We went on and there was this awkward silence until the screaming started again. The entire audience burst into tears, tugged at its mum's sleeve and demanded to be taken to the toilet."

"My Iron Lung" and an acoustic version of "Fake Plastic Trees" found their way onto the soundtrack of *Clueless*, Amy Heckerling's 1995 American college take on Jane Austen's *Emma*. In the film, "Fake Plastic Trees" was dismissed as "cry-baby music." Thom's response was almost Stipeian: "Cool. I am the moaning cry-baby from hell, really." Soon, though, it was time to look to the future.

Already, new songs "No Surprises" and "Subterranean Homesick Alien" had been integrated into their set and Radiohead mavens began to understand that "The Bends II" was no more ahoy than *The Bends* itself had contained "Creep II." "We could fall back on doing another moribund, miserable and negative record," mused Thom in December, revealing his true feelings vis-à-vis *The Bends*, "but I don't want to." Once again, his words would prove to be prescient.

Radiohead bade farewell to *The Bends* with the surprisingly success-ful "Street Spirit (Fade Out)" single in January 1996. Thom even turned up at the BRITs to collect the Freddie Mercury Award for *The Help Album* alongside Brian Eno. Radiohead were nominated for three awards: British Group; British Album of the Year; and British Video of the Year, for "Just." They won nothing and, never too well disguised, out came

Thom's competitive side. "Of course it bothered me that Oasis got loads of awards and we got none," he thundered to *Ray Gun*, before giving the ceremony an end-of-civilization hue. "I was sitting in a world of ugly men in suits accompanied by women who weren't their wives. All the bands were so far gone they didn't have a clue what they were saying."

"The Bends *was an incredibly personal album, which is why I spent most of my time denying it was personal at all.*" THOM

Radiohead's sense of humor is an acquired taste, but it's always 'bubbling ...'

5
"ONE OF THE GREATEST ALBUMS IN LIVING MEMORY"

For Radiohead's third album, Parlophone were smart enough not to trouble themselves with deadlines. Still postponing what needed to be done, a grueling North American tour in March notwithstanding, the band trod water for the first six months of 1996, other than announcing their support for the Rock the Vote campaign.

Phil stayed at home. Strangely for one who was no fan of traveling, Thom wandered around Europe, admitting to *Rolling Stone*: "I was basically catatonic . . . the claustrophobia . . . just having no sense of reality at all." Later it would sometimes seem that his solo career was just an excuse to tour. Jonny read even more books. Meanwhile, Ed moved to Islington, North London and went to India for a month. On his return, "There was a totally different vibe to us." Radiohead were ready to get back to work.

This time, there would be no John Leckie. His work was done. Once Scott Litt, R.E.M.'s long-term producer, changed his mind after offering his services, they looked inwards. Having impressed on "Black Star" and "Lucky," it was time for John Leckie's engineer Nigel Godrich to step up, despite never having actually produced an album. After it, he still hadn't, formally: the credits would read "committed to tape by Nigel Godrich with Radiohead."

"We thought this self-producing lark was a piece of piss," shrugged Ed. "The producer is there to pull you up when things are going wrong. We had to learn the non-musical side, the discipline."

In June, they returned to Canned Applause and began the album provisionally titled "Ones & Zeroes," rehearsing hard, before overanalyzing the results each day. It was still the enemy of luxury, but now Canned Applause had a Nintendo, somewhere. They decided to splash out on new equipment to the tune of $140,000, but actually spending such sums were beyond Nigel Godrich. Just as they had underspent their clothing allowance a few years ago, they underspent here: never let it be said that Radiohead fritter their money away.

In July, there were two dates in Oxford, quiet warm-ups for festivals including T in the Park. In August, there was yet another trip to America, this time lucratively opening for Alanis Morissette: "It was fun," recalled Jonny, "playing for thirteen-year-old girls and doing a Pink Floyd in front of them." They slipped in more new material such as "Karma Police" and "Climbing up the Walls," "Electioneering" and "Paranoid Android." Lovely Alanis Morissette covered "Creep" and "Fake Plastic Trees," but the sense of drift was almost palpable.

What were they to do? Nobody needed to tell them how great *The Bends* was anymore, but they hadn't outgrown it as they had *Pablo Honey*. Even so, they had toured *The Bends* to success and to death, especially in the United States. They needed to do something different, but what? Scarred by making *The Bends*, a new way to record was as important as a new musical direction. They tried a mobile studio: "Me and Jonny were nostalgic for a time we used to do 4-track stuff when we felt like it," sighed Thom, but those days were long gone.

The new material was different, but it was cluttered and far from coherent, and at Canned Applause they would break whatever spell they had cast by going home at the end of the day like sales assistants. Two months of toil brought just four nearly completed songs.

In September, Nigel Godrich had an idea to break the logjam and they decamped to St Catherine's Court, a sixteenth-century mansion north of the spa city of Bath. Since 1984, it had been owned by the actress Jane Seymour. The studio had been used previously by

Johnny Cash, New Order, and The Cure, much to the annoyance of the neighbors.

Thom promised whatever "a very grateful record" might be (in fairness this did evolve into "a record for the end of the world"), but he had decided that his voice need not be so central to the songs and that each track on the album could be sung in a different voice, inhabiting a different character. "He has a hang-up about his voice," sighed Ed. "But the fucker can sing anything and reduce you to tears."

Jonny played more keyboards than he had in years and sought a more improvisatory atmosphere. "Climbing Up the Walls" was the first to emerge in something approaching a finished state. They played in the ballroom; they recorded in the library and, in Phil's case, in children's bedrooms surrounded by cuddly toys, aided by reverb (they bought an EMT 140 plate reverb from that most underrated songwriter, Jona Lewie), echo, and even guitar effects pedals. When night fell, they played croquet, which was good for Thom, since those nights were too quiet for the city boy to sleep properly.

A valley in the Somerset countryside was not Thom's natural milieu. "I had a complete fever, it was like being ill all the time," he told *Addicted to Noise*. "It was the biggest fucking buzz and it was totally terrifying. Everything reminded you of your own mortality."

The house was haunted. Of course the house was haunted. "After a night of hearing voices, I got up and needed to cut my hair," claimed Thom. "I cut it with a penknife and went downstairs. Everyone asked if I was alright. I just said, 'What's wrong?'. Very gently, Phil took me aside and shaved it all off."

"Lucky" had shown Radiohead could work to order and when the opportunity came to contribute to Baz Luhrmann's *Romeo + Juliet*, after they had received the film's final thirty minutes while supporting Alanis Morissette, they took the bait. As it happened, Luhrmann was preaching to the converted, for Thom had seen Franco Zeffirelli's Oscar-nominated 1968 version when he was thirteen and bawled his eyes out, unable to understand why the lovers failed to flee. With an irony Alanis Morissette herself would have relished, "Exit Music (For a Film)" turned out to be just that, appearing only in the final credits. It was a Radiohead take on the doomed lovers, suicide pact and all, and Thom recorded his vocals in St Catherine's cold stone courtyard. There was a Johnny Cash-esque twang, an Ennio Morricone-style sweep, and such perceived similarity to "Crucified," by Swedish campers Army of Lovers that a court case was briefly mooted. It deserved more: "Every note of it made my head spin," enthused Thom to *Mojo*. "It was something I could turn up really loud and not wince at any moment."

The song did make a memorable appearance in the finale to the band-approved Irish comedy series *Father Ted*, when Ted attempts to alleviate Father Kevin's suicidal tendencies. Eddy and the Soul Band's chirpy version of "Theme from *Shaft*" does the trick until "Exit Music (For a Film)" sends Kevin spiraling down again. In time, it directly influenced others: Omar Robert Hamilton's novel of the Egyptian revolution, *The City Always Wins*, used the "we hope that you choke" refrain and, as The Hold Steady's Tad Kubler told *Classic Rock*, it spawned their 2014 opus "Oaks": "It came out of my total obsession with Radiohead's 'Exit Music (For a Film),' by how well they do that very cinematic thing."

Alternatively, while "Talk Show Host" wouldn't make the third album, it did make the *Romeo + Juliet* soundtrack, albeit radically remixed by Massive Attack. Indeed, there would subsequently be tentative moves towards the Bristol collective remixing the whole album, but as their Daddy G noted, "You have to treat it with a lot of respect. It would have taken us six months." It was Radiohead's most overtly trip hop moment and would enjoy occasional live resurrections.

They were absorbing the world around them. Jonny was discovering the delights of the mellotron and of tape loops, while rediscovering the work of his Abingdon crush Krzysztof Penderecki. He had turned Thom on to the drums and piano of Miles Davis's brutal, beautiful *Bitches Brew* (another legacy of Terence Gilmore-James, who remembered Thom as being "forlorn and a little isolated"), especially during the recording of "Subterranean Homesick Angel," among the usual mélange of Elvis Costello, Marvin Gaye, *Pet Sounds*, Can, Kraftwerk, Björk, and the novels of Thomas Pynchon.

There were other shapers of Radiohead's world, too: an intellectual cornerstone of Tony Blair's thrice-elected UK government, Will Hutton's *The State We're In* was a blistering if blustering critique of Britain under Margaret Thatcher; Edward S. Herman and Noam Chomsky's *Manufacturing Consent: The Political Economy of the Mass Media* equated American mass media with capitalism-bolstering propaganda; and there was Magnus Carlsson's adult cartoon *Robin*, where the protagonist is an unemployed Swede whose chum Benjamin is an alcoholic. No wonder the band's minds and music were so cluttered. All the same, by Christmas, much to their own surprise, they were there or, more accurately, thereabouts. "We had the best time doing that record. The possibilities seemed endless," said Thom many years later. In truth he was drained, but not nearly as drained as he was going to be. "I said I couldn't do the Glastonbury date we were supposed to do. I was burned out, I needed a break. I didn't get one for a year and a half, by which time I was catatonic."

Thereabouts eventually became there. The masses of song fragments had been culled, clipped, and honed, but the album was still too long. The angry "Polyethylene" and the more lonesome "A Reminder," with its announcements from the Prague Metro, were defenestrated to B-sides at the last minute. This left twelve songs which formed a whole rather than individual entities. Perhaps, though, the most crucial decision had been made earlier when live favorite and the album's most poppy moment, "Lift," had been dropped.

A decade later, Ed was still relieved. "We subconsciously killed it. It was a big anthemic song. If 'Lift' had been on the album, it would have taken us to a different place. We'd probably have sold a lot more records, but it would have killed us."

The album was rechristened. A lackluster Pixies-esque trundle called "OK Computer" was never a serious contender for the album, although as "Palo Alto" it eventually became a "No Surprises" B-side. Its title, though, taken from the television version of Douglas Adams's *The Hitchhiker's Guide to the Galaxy*, when the two-headed, three-armed Zaphod Beeblebrox character says, "Okay computer, I want full manual control now," had resonance and it stuck.

What running order would best showcase these entwined songs? For most bands and most albums, it's usually a question quickly answered. Some even write openers and closers to order; some frontload with singles, both sins Radiohead could never be accused of.

With a May 1997 release date penciled in for Japan, and June everywhere else, Thom took it upon himself to decide that running order, replaying the album in combination after combination. Initially, the others chipped in, since it wasn't clear what should go where and how the narrative arc they all felt was there in theory would unfurl in practice. "I don't think you realize how vital running order is until you fuck it up, like we did with the first record," explained Ed. "For *OK Computer* it was a nightmare. It was like bloody horse-trading."

Weeks passed, as did a bacchanalian Dublin evening with U2 at the *Hot Press* Awards in February. Bono and Thom would become friends, but Thom was aghast when Bono and Republican senator John Kasich bonded over Radiohead: "Bad guys like our music too?"

One by one the others lost interest to the point where Thom felt he was being ignored. The others ignored that feeling too. Soon, EMI consulted their calendars and got twitchy. This was meant to be the year Oasis reconquered the UK (and perhaps the US, although in hindsight that was never going to happen) with the follow-up to *(What's The Story) Morning Glory?*. Everything else was assumed to be chasing second place. It wouldn't have turned out like that, even if the Oasis album had been great. By the time Oasis's *Be Here Now* was released, eight weeks after *OK Computer*, Oasis had already self-sabotaged with an album of dreary stodge.

Eventually, Thom was happy. But he was right to tarry. *OK Computer* would be perfectly sequenced, everything in its right place: the inexorable descent into track seven, "Fitter Happier," and the slow resuscitation afterwards, with moments of anguish and some jokes. What now?

Drained or not, Thom joined another band, albeit an imaginary one, The Venus in Furs, alongside Jonny; Jonny's guitar soulmate Bernard Butler; Roxy Music's Andy Mackay; and David Gray's rather excitable percussionist, Craig "Clune" McClune. They were assembled for the Michael Stipe-produced Ewan McGregor vehicle, *Velvet Goldmine*, which was roughly based on the David Bowie/Iggy Pop relationship and wouldn't be premiered until late 1998. On the soundtrack, Thom sang fairly faithful versions of Roxy Music's "2HB," "Ladytron," and "Bitter-Sweet," while the band backed actor Jonathan Rhys Meyers's serviceable crack at Brian Eno's "Baby's on Fire" and Cockney Rebel's glorious "Tumbling Down."

On the Radiohead front, Parlophone cannot have sensed a second *The Bends*, but what did they actually expect? They had given Radiohead the budget (although even they baulked at plans to make a video for every song) and the time to make the album the band needed to make. Naturally, EMI had heard the works in progress both live and in the studio, but this? It didn't sound finished. It certainly didn't sound hit-laden and, quietly, Capitol reduced the initial US pressing run from two million to 500,000. Years later, having one of the greatest albums of the twentieth century dropped into their laps and not noticing seems negligent, the age-old saga of The Man not getting The Talent, but EMI deserve some slack. This was music from outer space and the label would cotton on with alacrity, long before the reviews tumbled in.

The sleeve would be another Thom (in White Chocolate Farm guise) and Stanley Donwood collaboration. Indeed, Stanley Donwood had spent an extended period with the group at Jane Seymour's place. The pair used a tablet, a light pen, and a "no erasing" rule to craft a sprawling cornucopia of ideas. The blurring of the junction on the front (the eastbound I-84 in Hartford, Connecticut) suggests the idea of a fork in the career was illusionary, but the key for Thom was found on the reverse of the back cover, an ancient sign which to him meant No Demons Allowed. Had the phrase not made them sound like Swedish death metallers, it might have made a better album title. For Thom, Radiohead have always been about banishing demons. It didn't look like anything else, but it looked fabulous: mission successful. "I was incredibly happy with the artwork," admitted Stanley Donwood. "But then I had grave doubts."

Radiohead had always enjoyed Barcelona, so with expectations rising and a UK release date of June 16, and an American one of July 1, now set in stone, they launched the album there in May, following three low-key Lisbon dates. In the first and last Radiohead press shindig, journalists from across the world (just two from the United States though) were invited to hear the album, talk to the band, and see them play. Thom had long tired of being interrogated, but everyone was unsure of how the album would perform, so they needed to perform for the media. The scales were about to tilt: where once Radiohead needed the press to sell records and tickets; now the press would need Radiohead to sell copies of newspapers and magazines. After this last blow-out, they would be more elusive and more exclusive.

The clattering opener, "Airbag," was a gripping statement of intent. Phil had discovered the Mo' Wax label, especially their star-turn DJ Shadow, whose cut-up technique he emulated ("How that man pastes rhythms to each other," the drummer gushed), programming his drum sounds and placing them in the backing track through Jonny's guitar pedals. Even the original title, "Last Night an Airbag Saved My Life," was a cut-up, merging Indeep's 1982 hit, "Last Night a D.J. Saved My Life" with "An Airbag Saved My Life," a headline Thom had seen in a car magazine. The loose car-crash theme is based on Thom's pre-Exeter car-wrecking collision, still the source of his driving angst ("Nothing scares me more than driving; I hate it with a fucking passion."), but there were also hints of *The Tibetan Book of Living and Dying* by later-disgraced lama Sogyal Rinpoche, which Thom couldn't finish—"It freaked the living crap out of me." Colin's assured bass was almost funky, the first fruits of the lessons he'd been taking since *The Bends*. Ed's guitar nodded to Robert Fripp on King Crimson's *Red* album, and Jonny's guitar was tremolo-enhanced. In the best possible sense, it was a mess, an exhilarating, inspired mess.

The Hitchhiker's Guide to the Galaxy appeared again in "Paranoid Android," from the book/show's most durable character, Marvin the Paranoid Android. There would be dozens of versions, some lasting for over fifteen minutes, as they attempted to fertilize Queen's "Bohemian Rhapsody," The Beatles' "Happiness Is a Warm Gun," Pixies, DJ Shadow, Ennio Morricone, and Can. The final incarnation, selected by Phil, lasts for just six minutes twenty-three seconds until its abrupt finish. When they came to record one of the three sections in the St Catherine's Court ballroom, they lit candles, sipped vodka and orange, and for the first time in their career, jammed to record.

According to Thom, the idea for "Paranoid Android" had festered since he went for a quiet drink in Los Angeles at some upmarket bar he's never named, so it may be fictional or, more likely, the hotel where he was staying. There, "surrounded by parasites, the dullest fucking people on earth," everyone (bar Thom, naturally) had hoovered up industrial quantities of cocaine, including the "kicking squalling Gucci little piggy" who turned into a demon after her drink had been spilled. Back in his hotel room at 5am, Thom wrote much of the saga.

The end result, featuring Ed on clavinet, cascaded like Radiohead had never cascaded before, and to Ed it was "to 'Bohemian Rhapsody' what 'Creep' was to Scott Walker." And, quite rightly, he found it very funny indeed. "I like songs that have a universe inside them," explained Colin, "loud and soft, pretty and ugly, fast and slow. 'Paranoid Android' is all those things. It's wild and savage, something we did when we didn't know how to do anything and there were no rules."

Magnus Carlsson of *Robin* fame made the video—his first. MTV censored the nipples, but as Jonny rued, "They left in the stuff where a man's sawing through his own limbs." As if to show there can be justice in the world, even daytime Radio 1 adored it, and it reached No. 3 in the British charts. It's still their highest placing.

From *Highway 61 Revisited*, Bob Dylan's lyrics diverged into angry allegory, always leaving room for interpretation, but always with an undertow of fury. Nobody ever called Thom Yorke a New Bob Dylan, but the pair walk some of the same road, sharing more than a willingness to exhume both obscure and familiar back catalog live. They reinterpret material as their sense of adventure takes them and they reinvent themselves when and how they see fit.

In title alone, *OK Computer*'s oldest song, "Subterranean Homesick Alien," was an overt nod to Bob Dylan's "Subterranean Homesick Blues." "It's like the Dylan song, but not," noted Thom, in best Dylanese, before pretending it was "a joke song." Originally titled "Uptight," written by Thom during *The Bends* era and performed by him and Jonny acoustically, before being reworked with Thom on piano, it evolved into a more esoteric direction for *OK Computer*. It's a stream of consciousness, detailing on the one hand, an alien's bemused visit to suburban Earth and, on the other, the perennial Radiohead theme that what gets built up is quite likely to be torn down.

For all his vocal tics, in an alternative world Thom would have made a most effective crooner. He may yet be tempted. As Thom doubtless knows, crooning, as much as electronic music or sampling or cut-ups, was only made possible by technical advance. Before vocal amplification via microphone, live singing was a question of reaching the back row by bellow or, should you be an opera singer, projection. Suddenly, it was possible to vary the tone, to establish some sort of intimacy. Rudy Vallée or Al Bowlly could be there with you in your kitchen via the magic of radio, and if the radio show was Bing Crosby's, it would have been prerecorded and then edited—cut up, if you will—to provide the best aural experience. Meanwhile in the studio, Crosby, the first pop star, was also the first man to master his recordings onto magnetic tape and to understand how the placing of microphones affected what the listeners hear. Should Thom overtly unleash his inner croon, he's only repaying a debt.

Perhaps because it's so obviously conventional, "Let Down" is rarely mentioned as an *OK Computer* peak, but it's unquestionably up there. Moreover, it's crucial evidence in the Thom The Crooner? debate. Colin and Ed always agreed that it was their Frank Sinatra meets Joy Division moment. The layered, tracked vocals turn Thom into sadder versions of both Phil and Don Everly, and when he sings "Don't get sentimental: it always ends up drivel," it's a reminder to himself to avoid vicarious emotionalizing. Unusual among a Radiohead song finished in the wee small hours—3am in St. Catherine's ballroom—it doesn't sound like it. The aching, elegiac melody would have made an interesting, career-diverting single and it was scheduled as such, but the band didn't like the video, which, unusually, featured them. They paid £50,000 of their own money for it to be scrapped. Shame.

Radiohead's sense of humor is an acquired taste, but it's always bubbling. "Karma Police" was both a band in-joke and part of their guarding against the demons which wealth and power might unfetter. More succinctly, karma police meant that if you do something bad or behave insensitively, you'll receive some sort of justice. Ed thought the joke might form the basis for a song. "It's not entirely serious," noted Thom plaintively to Q. "I hope people realize that." There's a threat of course, but it's a wry threat and at the very end, the scratching sound is Nigel Godrich turning off Ed's guitar delay pedal. Director Jonathan Glazer had originally pitched the idea of a video based on the opening credits to David Lynch's *Lost Highway* to Marilyn Manson for "Long Hard Road Out of Hell." Marilyn Manson turned it down; Radiohead embraced the idea and it was nominated for four MTV video awards in 1998. The karma police on patrol.

Although only lasting one minute fifty-seven seconds, "Fitter Happier" is *OK Computer*'s centerpiece; literally and emotionally. Initially mooted as an album opener, it opened dates on the subsequent tour. The voice is that of Fred Cooper, the synthesized voice for the Apple Macintosh's SimpleText application, as utilized by Stephen Hawking, and here spliced together by Thom. Curiously, Thom reckoned it was "the most upsetting thing I've written," and while it wasn't clear how much he was joking—its guide to a more fulfilling life overlaps new friend Baz Luhrmann's "Everybody's Free (To Wear Sunscreen)"—the disembodied voice being overwhelmed by plangent piano exudes a certain drowning helplessness. More curious still, the sleeve claimed the BBC nature program, *The Flight of the Condor* had been sampled. It hadn't: Thom taped the 1975 conspiracy thriller *Three Days of the Condor* off the television and used a sample of dialogue in "Fitter Happier": "this is the panic office." In

2015, Stanley Donwood's 25-year retrospective, ambiently soundtracked by Thom, would be titled *The Panic Office*.

Thom's sterling work on the running order reached its zenith when "Fitter Happier" segued into the tambourine rattle and distorted guitar twang of "Electioneering" and began the second half of the *OK Computer* equation. Musically, it was *OK Computer*'s hard-rocker, perhaps the only moment in popular music history where R.E.M.'s *Monster* was a genuine influence. Unusually for Radiohead and for *OK Computer*, it made the cut in almost identical form to the very earliest demos. As befits its title, this was the album's most overtly political moment, with undertows of Will Hutton, of Noam Chomsky, and of Eric Hobsbawm's communist reading of the twentieth century, *The Age of Extremes*. It's a cynical take on politics, specifically the UK's Poll Tax riots of 1990. More generally, it evoked "riot sheelds" (*sic*), "voodoo economicks" (*sic*), and the far from unfamiliar notion that politicians will do anything to get elected. But it's also about Radiohead: selling themselves across the globe, a world where "buy my record" = "vote for me."

Leonard Cohen always said that the key to understanding "First We Take Manhattan" was to accept that the narrator is insane. The same applies to "Climbing up the Walls" with its explicit suggestion of cartoon horror-flick domestic violence. Possibly joking, Thom told *Q* he had originally seen *OK Computer* as "an album you could sit down and eat to in a nice restaurant." "Climbing up the Walls" put paid to that notion. This was the song that had given Alanis Morissette's young audience the heebie-jeebies, when it lasted for fifteen minutes and featured a lengthy Jonny organ solo as Thom wailed "the walls, the walls." Unsurprisingly, it was inspired by Thom's time as a mental hospital orderly, and when he revisited some old fragments of lyric during R.E.M. tour downtime, the song began to take shape.

Recorded during a hailstorm, the results were genuinely sinister, even more so when it came to the ending, one long-hold discordant note played by sixteen violins in homage to Krzysztof Penderecki. "It's a block of white noise," explained Jonny, who played xylophone, although Colin would never be impressed. "And it happens when sixteen violins are playing quarter tones apart. It's the most frightening sound, but it's beautiful." In live performance Jonny would tune into and play "random" classical and talk radio stations. They weren't random at all, of course, but preselected. "I don't want 'The Size of a Cow' to come out," he noted, understandably enough.

In 2019, "Climbing up the Walls" featured in the fifth series of the BBC's widely acclaimed *Peaky Blinders*, following "Pyramid Song," "You and Whose Army?," "Life in a Glasshouse," and "I Might Be Wrong." The scene involved dark, power-based sex. The show's star, Cillian Murphy, helped construct the soundtrack: "I've been a huge fan since I was a teenager," he told *Spin*. "To be given access to such an incredible back catalog is a huge honor."

Recording was difficult, but "No Surprises" was easiness itself once they had decided that the pace would be funereal. There were six versions made, but they returned to the first for *OK Computer*. "We pressed the button, the red light came on and there was 'No Surprises,'" Thom told *Mojo*. The album's most *Pet Sounds* moment, Ed thought it harkened to Louis Armstrong's "What a Wonderful World," but these are adult lyrics about the minutiae of adult situations and the drudgery of the suburban life that so terrified Thom. Some divine backing vocals made it both more serene and more paranoid.

Those looking for where Radiohead were going next would find no clues in the closing "The Tourist," which marked Jonny's most significant songwriting contribution since *Pablo Honey* and, ever modest, he was surprised the others were so keen on it. Based around him observing

OK COMPUTER

RECORDED AT Canned Applause, Didcot; St Catherine's Court, Bath

PRODUCED BY Nigel Godrich & Radiohead

PERSONNEL
Colin Greenwood
Ed O'Brien
Jonny Greenwood
Phil Selway
Thom Yorke

COVER ART
Stanley Donwood: pictures
The White Chocolate Farm: pictures

RELEASED Jun 16, 1997

LABEL Parlophone, CDNODATA 02

HIGHEST CHART POSITION ON RELEASE UK 1, US 21, GER 27, FRA 3, NL 2, NZ 1, SWE 3, CAN 2, SWI 40, SPA 42, AUS 7

TRACK LIST
Airbag
Paranoid Android
Subterranean Homesick Alien
Exit Music (For a Film)
Let Down
Karma Police
Fitter Happier
Electioneering
Climbing up the Walls
No Surprises
Lucky
The Tourist

"We had the best time doing that record. The possibilities seemed endless." THOM

rushed, schedule-packing American tourists in France, it's a finale in the tradition of (but superior to) *The White Album*'s Ringo Starr-sung "Goodnight." With Phil's drums at their most tender, it's a tension-releasing comedown after the preceding intensity.

Thom played no instruments on the track and claimed not to remember his one-take vocals. "I had been told to sing a rough vocal so we could work on it," he told Q. "There's no emotional involvement." Frankly, it's hard to take him seriously, although maybe he was stepping aside to allow Jonny to take the spotlight. Either way, it's the denouement *OK Computer* deserves. The final, decisive "ping" is a perfect full stop, and the car that seems out of control at the end might just lead into the crash that begins "Airbag": If so, the circle is complete.

The years have been kind to *OK Computer*, which Thom claims was written from the viewpoint of someone outside, looking in. "We were living in orbit, on a bus, so when you stepped back into the real world it didn't compute. I felt very little connection with my fellow human beings."

It is so multilayered, so intriguing, so laden with emotional and witty trip wires that it yields new treasures with every listen, thus avoiding the trap of overfamiliarity which "Bohemian Rhapsody" tumbled into, but its spawn "Paranoid Android" has avoided. Sure, nobody need hear "Fitter Happier" again, but that interlude was always uneasy listening. Hindsight tells us there is something overly crude about how "Electioneering" jackhammers. Moreover, Thom's railing against the misdeeds of Tony Blair and George W. Bush would be overtaken by darker deeds and darker people and today his gripes seem quaint rather than angry. Depth and beauty are timeless, though, and so, for all the mostly misguided suggestions that *OK Computer* was prog rock or art-rock ("Oh God, what a ghastly thought," winced Colin), it stands alone. As we now know, Radiohead chose not to redo it. For all that *OK Computer* shifted music's tectonic plates, and for all that many have tried, nobody has made a record which remotely sounds like it. Not even Radiohead.

Thom's fear that "we had blown it" proved to be wildly wide of the mark and the acclaim was almost universal. Soon Thom would visit Ed's chiropractor father who would work all kinds of hands-on magic and increase the singer's height by an inch to five foot five. And Ed's father, the biggest musical fan of all the extended tribe, decided that *OK Computer* was a classic after just five listens. The *NME* was on the case with remarkable foresight, giving *OK Computer* 10/10 and pronouncing it "one of the greatest albums in living memory." Jonny was cautious in his appraisal: "I don't think it's that good. There are good songs, but there are songs that sound like dead ends. We haven't finished yet."

Q: how do you follow OK Computer?
A: you don't even try.

6
OK? NOT OK

W hat to do? Another level of success brought rewards as well as pressure. The previous tour had finished in August 1996 in Clarkston, Michigan, and the nine months until those three low-key *OK Computer* warm-up dates at Lisbon's Garage had been their longest break from performance. Never again would Radiohead feel compelled to tour every nook and cranny that would have them, but sometimes it still felt like it: the dates in support of *OK Computer* would almost pull the band apart and come closer still to breaking Thom. Now the scale would be bigger and the scope for fertile imaginations had widened immeasurably, but they remained road hogs: In 1997, the year of their ascension into the land of giants, they played eighty-six shows from the middle of May to the middle of November.

The week before *OK Computer* reached No. 1 in the UK, they chose to perform a six-song set at the Tibetan Freedom Concert at the Downing Stadium on Randalls Island, in New York's East River. Organized by The Beastie Boys, it featured a raft of the concerned, including U2, Blur, Noel Gallagher, Björk and The Foo Fighters. Before "The Bends," Thom railed at multinationals exploiting Tibet and so began his evolution into concerted activism.

After the show, Colin met American author and literary critic Molly McGrann, who was studying for her masters. They were soon an item: "Shortly afterwards she came over. When I took her to the Aziz restaurant on the Cowley Road, she decided she liked Oxford."

Six days later, as if to confirm the Aziz patrons were breathing more rarefied air, Madonna, Courtney Love, Lenny Kravitz, and Marilyn Manson attended a New York show. Tom Cruise (Tom Cruise!) and Brad Pitt turned up to the Troubadour in Los Angeles.

A week before they headlined Glastonbury (Thom's objections had long been overruled), Radiohead played to 33,000 at Dublin's RDS Arena, their largest headliner to date. Since the R.E.M. shows, Radiohead had become comfortable on the big stage, playing for big crowds who didn't even have to be their own. Before Dublin, the band were edgy though. Already admitting to feeling "pure blind terror," Thom had some sort of out-of-body, waking dream experience, a saga which would find its way into "How to Disappear Completely." The show? Excellent of course. And when Thom declared, "It's karaoke time," "Creep," their golden albatross, took flight.

The signal event of the immediate fallout took place in the fields of Glastonbury. Their first English date since *OK Computer* had captivated and enthralled, and headlining the Pyramid Stage on Saturday evening ought to have been the confirmation that 1997 belonged to them, even if Ed was later heard to muse at the Q Awards that R.O.C.'s *Virgin* and Belle & Sebastian's *If You're Feeling Sinister* were superior albums. In fairness, the R.O.C. album did include Idi Amin's laugh: Even *OK Computer* couldn't compete with that.

Things began well, with a gripping opening salvo of "Lucky," "My Iron Lung," and "Airbag" making Thom's reasons to be fearful seem spurious. As "Paranoid Android" began, Thom's monitors gave up and he could no longer hear what he was singing or what the band were playing. The set began to slalom out of control. During "Talk Show Host," some of the lighting went down. Thom was ready to walk off, killing the momentum and further exposing their humiliation. Thom told *NME* he had sidled over to Ed and said: "I'm off mate, see you later." Ed sagaciously responded: "If you do, you'll probably spend the rest of your life regretting it." Instead, Thom embraced his inner Bruce Dickinson and rallied, bellowing "I haven't been able to see one person in the crowd the whole set. I want to see you lot." The lights swung onto the audience.

As far as Thom's good eye could see, there were tens of thousands of people enjoying a Somerset evening in the heart of Britain's countryside. They were enjoying Radiohead even more. Thom seized the moment, seized his band's destiny, and with atypical overstatement declared the rest of the performance "the most important hour in our lives."

That was as good as it got. Having reached the mountain top, they could go no higher, and after that special night Thom admitted, "Everything was a let-down." Ed slumped into depression ("I was in the best band in the world, we'd made a record I was so, so proud of, but I was so unhappy and I felt so alone."), which a solo trip to Brazil and his discovery of that nation's music (Jorge Ben especially), alongside a boxing-based fitness regime, helped conquer.

The United States beckoned yet again, this time with Phil's favorites Teenage Fanclub in support. A combination of word of mouth and airplay, allied to the goodwill *The Bends* album and ceaseless touring had generated, propelled *OK Computer* to double platinum status, albeit only to No. 21 in the charts. A new song, "Motion Picture Soundtrack," was occasionally aired.

The tour began with *The Tonight Show with Jay Leno* in Los Angeles and ended with *The Late Show with David Letterman* in New York, where, the previous night, Thom had apologized to the Hammerstein Ballroom crowd for being tired. In July, in San Francisco, Thom even found time to co-write and guest on UNKLE's "Rabbit in Your Headlights," which won 1999's MVPA (Music Video Production Association) Best International Video Award and was the highlight of DJ Shadow and Warp label boss James Lavelle's overhyped, under-satisfying project.

Back home, there was—new, expanded scale notwithstanding—a

smaller fan club date at the Astoria which the band loved as they redis-covered obscurities and hidden gems ("Maquiladora," "Banana Co," even "Lurgee") with the exact people who needed to hear them redis-covered. There was a mid-level date in Brixton which Thom hated and, after another European trek, a sell-out at Wembley Arena. As a reminder of just how fragile Thom was becoming, Wembley preceded a show at Birmingham NEC where he disappeared after the soundcheck and found himself on a train full of gig-bound fans. "That was the closest I came to escaping," he told *NME*. He was still frazzled after the show and the trauma would be detailed on *Kid A*'s "Everything in Its Right Place." From there, for Thom, it was downhill all the way.

At the end of the year, Thom explained to the inner circle that he was withdrawing from the media. True, it was an opportunity to build mystique, but he was being crushed by the whole circus. The media responded by anointing Radiohead as Band of the Year in *Rolling Stone*, while *OK Computer* was Album of the Year in *Q* and in second place in *NME* (behind Spiritualized's *Ladies and Gentlemen We Are Floating in Space*) and *Spin* (behind Cornershop's *When I Was Born for the 7th Time*). The scales hadn't been tilted, they had been overturned.

The same old question: what now? Thom knew what he didn't want: "I've no intention of doing fucking aural soundscapes or whatever. It's not gonna happen." The jump from *Pablo Honey* to *The Bends* had been giant, but the albums were clearly the work of the same, albeit rapidly improving, band. The leap from *The Bends* to *OK Computer* was from one dimension to another. As 1998 dawned, they wanted—"needed" might still have been a more apposite word—to maintain their success, but they would not remake *OK Computer*. That didn't mean they had any ideas beyond kicking against the accepted notions of what a globally success-ful pop group should do, but as Ed told *Q*, "The day we make a record that's a happy affair is the day we make a shit album."

They did what they always did when they were short of ideas: they fudged. Thom provided backing vocals to labelmates Sparklehorse's B-side version of Pink Floyd's "Wish You Were Here." In January and February, they hauled themselves back to Japan for some miserable dates and for some more pleasant ones in Australasia. They even aired another inchoate song, provisionally entitled "Big Ideas (Don't Get Any)," which Thom performed solo and acoustically in Tokyo. Much later, it would be rechristened "Nude." It sounded like what it was: a work very much in progress, but it certainly didn't sound like *OK Computer*.

Yet again, America called and in April the revealingly titled "How to Disappear Completely and Not Be Found" was aired in front of Nigel Godrich, who was in Los Angeles attempting to do some road recording. The title came from Doug Richmond's 1985 book, a guide to creating a new identity after faking suicide, but, intriguingly, in 1993 Thom had been asked by *NME* what the band were going to do after touring *Pablo Honey*. He replied, "We're going to disappear completely." For reasons never fully explained, Ed thought the next album might have a more Motown or Stax or Smiths bent. He also assumed it would be packed with three-minute guitar songs, but he appears not to have mentioned this to the rest of the group. Radiohead were at a creative full stop unlike any they had encountered before.

Part of the problem was Thom. That swiftly jettisoned idea of *OK Computer*'s twelve songs in twelve vocal styles was a yearning hiding in plain sight. For all that, on the outside, things couldn't have gone better vis-à-vis *OK Computer*, the man who once said "Songwriting is therapy for me," was afflicted by writer's block and on the verge of a breakdown, withered by the relentless touring schedule, the necessity to creatively water-tread while promoting *OK Computer*, and that sense of misplaced guilt he has never been able to shed.

The angst, the "pervading sense of loneliness I've had since the day I was born," which he confessed to *Rolling Stone* in 1995, had unquestionably resurfaced, but there are many Thoms. He's not without petulance ("I'm always losing my temper"), but he's sufficiently detached to chuckle at his own ludicrousness and he's fortunate to have bandmates who'll roll their eyes rather than raise their fists. "He's quite moody, quite childish and often aloof," noted Jonny carefully. "He's very volatile to be around and while he can be a miserable complainer, he's so excited and child-like in the studio."

Anyone who calls an album after a Jerky Boys sketch, has a song inspired by a Goons skit, and who dedicated an album to Bill Hicks is hardly Mr Permanently Miserable and, as Colin claimed, "Thom's a reasonably upbeat person, actually." None, though, described him as accurately as British newspaper *The Guardian*, who noted his sometimes juvenile sense of humor, his obsession with being an outsider, and his radical idealism: "He's a mass of contradictions, a strange blend of snide cynicism, bitter self-pity and earnest decency."

Meanwhile, in March, between tours of Australia and the United States, Radiohead reconvened to record a song, "Big Boots (Man-O-War)" for the film *The Avengers*, in the hope it would galvanize the new album as "Lucky" had kick-started *OK Computer*. It wasn't even new—originally meant for *The Bends*, then for a B-side, and then for *OK Computer*—the band completed the song yet again. Then they dumped it again. It wasn't good enough and their attempt to regenerate had backfired. They wouldn't let go though: as late as *A Moon Shaped Pool*, it was still under consideration, before it finally surfaced on *OKNOTOK 1997 2017*.

Thom had also discovered Brazilian-English art-rockers Drugstore and he duetted with singer Isabel Monteiro on their only hit, "El President." Drugstore were promptly dropped by their label and it was

Radiohead pass their Britpop audition. Bleached blond hair? Tick. Starry shirt? Tick.
Floppy fringe? Tick. Drummer's hairline just about hidden? Tick. Someone staring
moodily into the distance? Tick.

Jonny Greenwood: his moment, like his band's, would come after Pablo Honey.

A rare shot of Radiohead's brief spell as a sextet.

Glastonbury, 26 June, 1994. The t-shirt depicted Astro Boy (aka Mighty Atom), hero of Osamu Tezuka's manga series.

Ed (approaching pensive), Phil (pensive), Thom (even more pensive), Colin (mildly pensive), Jonny (post-pensive).

Thom: sinisterly detached.

Thom and Jonny performing at the Tibetan Freedom Concert, RFK Stadium, Washington D.C., USA, 14 June, 1998.

The older they got, the less inclined they were to compromise.

Ed on stage at the Santa Barbara Bowl, CA, USA, 29 June, 2001.

Jonny had evolved from being the kid at the side of the stage, to Radiohead's musical conscience.

Thom airing In Rainbows *tracks at the Hammersmith Apollo, London, 19 May, 2006.*

Ed and Thom at the Reading Festival, 30 August, 2009.

From left: Ed (broody), Jonny (fringy), Colin (wary), Thom (sleazy), Phil (Phily).

Nigel Godrich plays a Thom solo show at Sonar Festival, Barcelona, Spain, 16 June, 2018.

Phil and Ed being inducted into the Rock & Roll Hall of Fame at the Barclays Center, Brooklyn, NY, USA, March 29, 2019.

Thom solo at Piazza Colbert, Barolo, Italy, 16 July, 2019.

hard to escape the fact that Thom was drifting: "We've been running on bravado," he lamented, "it's all bollocks."

The awards kept flowing though. There was a first Grammy for Best Alternative Music Album for *OK Computer*, which also won *Q*'s Best Album Ever, and when "Karma Police" wasn't winning its Ivor Novello Award for Best Contemporary Song, "Paranoid Android" was winning one for the not wholly distinct Best Song Musically and Lyrically. By April 1998, as the American tour finished with two nights at Radio City Music Hall, *OK Computer* had achieved its first platinum status in the United States.

Before that, Michael Stipe had guested at the San Francisco show and much consternation was caused the previous day when Thom apparently consented to a rare interview at his old cheerleaders KROQ-FM. The deeply unpleasant DJ goaded Thom about his lazy eye and humiliated him into playing an acoustic version of "Creep," before Thom exploded in fury on air. The ensuing fight ended with Thom being taken to hospital. The evening's gig was in danger, much to the disappointment of irate fans who swamped the station's switchboard. The date—April 1—and the note-for-note similarity of "Creep" to a version Thom had played on the station some time ago ought to have been a clue that things weren't quite as they seemed and in-house prankster Ralph Garman swiftly outed himself as Thom's impersonator. No wonder the real Thom was struggling.

A brief, extras-free, will-this-do? video compilation, *7 Television Commercials*, kept things ticking over, and in June there was an even bigger Tibetan Freedom Concert, this time a two-nighter at Washington's 66,000-capacity RFK Stadium alongside a significantly more stellar lineup (Kraftwerk, Dave Matthews Band, Wyclef Jean) than 1997. Lightning stopped the first night (one woman suffered 20%, second-degree burns) before Radiohead appeared. "We had all this adrenaline and didn't know what to do with it," explained Thom to *Melody Maker*. They sloped off to play the eight-hundred-capacity 9.30 Club. Michael Stipe joined them on "Lucky."

Re-booked on the second RFK night, Radiohead were assisted by Michael Stipe again on "Lucky" and "Creep." Thom was so delighted he returned the favor during R.E.M.'s set, on "Be Mine," before taking Patti Smith's part on "E-Bow the Letter." A day later, Thom was at the Tibetan Freedom Rally, where he strummed an acoustic "Street Spirit (Fade Out)."

The euphoria didn't last. Thom's usual ailments, the general sickliness, the bitten fingernails, had resurfaced, but when the tour finally ground to a halt after the Tibet shows, he was broken. Nigel Godrich was in New York helping Michael Stipe mix R.E.M.'s *Up* album and, still potentially peripatetic, Thom arranged to visit from England, "because they're two of my favorite people in the world and I needed to do something." The pair loyally went to JFK to meet his plane, but there was no Thom. He'd set off for Heathrow, turned back and kept shtoom. "I was just so out of it. That day was a real low point for me because Michael was my fucking hero."

Sick of being stuck in Oxford drawing hawthorn hedges because they suggested a brain, Thom fled to Cornwall to deal with his mental health issues and, concomitantly, his writer's block. He took to writing on piano rather than guitar, he walked more than he'd walked before and, harkening to his Exeter days, he re-immersed himself in Sturm und Drang techno, this time Aphex Twin ("I don't really know anything about him," shrugged Colin, ominously) and Autechre from hardcore Sheffield dance label Warp. "The first time I heard 'Freeman, Hardy & Willis Acid,'" remembered Thom of the Aphex Twin/Squarepusher instrumental, "I was completely straight, but it was like someone had reached over and switched a switch in my head. I never, ever saw anything the same again." All the same, this was a dark period: "I was a complete fucking mess. Really, really ill."

In November, the documentary *Meeting People is Easy* was released. Directed by Grant Gee of "No Surprises" fame, it was an unblinking portrait of a band in a position to reap the rewards of all they had hoped and worked for. Yet, waylaid by a combination of frailty, stubbornness, guilt, and incomprehension, they simply couldn't deal with it. Grant Gee detailed the promotional merry-go-round of the *OK Computer* earthquake, the shows, the interviews, the day in the studio failing to capture "Big Boots (Man-O-War)" and the ennui of not merely being within the bubble, but being the bubble itself. It's compulsive viewing, and for all its unsparing detail, what was left on the cutting-room floor would have been more interesting viewing still. It sold half a million copies.

In December 1998, shortly after Colin, the man formerly known as "Shabba" (as in "Mr. Loverman"), married Molly McGrann at Oxford Registry Office (Jesse arrived in 2003, Asa in 2005, Henry in 2009), there was a Paris show to celebrate the fiftieth anniversary of the charity Amnesty International, alongside their old friend Alanis Morissette, Peter Gabriel, and Tracy Chapman. This time, there was no new material and, disappointingly, despite lengthy rehearsals, a plan to play Can's "The Thief" was scrapped at the last minute. It was their only European show of the year and it would be their last for eighteen months, other than 1999's Tibetan Freedom Concert.

By New Year's Eve, Thom was at his lowest ebb. "It was one the worst points in my life," he told *Q*. "I felt like I was going fucking crazy. Every time I picked up the guitar, I got the horrors. All melodies were pure embarrassment to me. I just wanted rhythm."

To cheer himself up, he purchased the rest of the Warp back catalog. Replenished by the uncompromising sounds of Squarepusher, Black Dog, LFO, and Boards of Canada, Thom gradually became fitter and happier. The way ahead began to take shape.

Jonny: he loves Jimmy Smith, he loves the Blade Runner *soundtrack, he loves Brian Eno and he loves Can.*

7
EVERYTHING IN ITS RIGHT PLACE AT LAST

Once again Parlophone were sufficiently savvy to avoid setting deadlines for the follow-up to *OK Computer*, but this time around, there would be no fashioning of new material at Canned Applause. Making a mistake Phil described as "very much a case of us tripping ourselves up," the band met in Paris, city of their most recent live appearance. For all that some new songs had been aired live, the blunt truth was that when they converged at Guillaume Tell Studios, other than "Lost at Sea" (dumped, but later resurrected as "In Limbo"), Thom had nothing beyond fragments, ideas, and nascent song shapes. His hope was that the others would build these snippets up into something usable. There were many band meetings.

"We started 30 or 40 things," winced Ed to *Q*. "But no decisions were made on any of them. You knee-jerk and then you panic." In March, they fled to Medley Studio in Copenhagen, or Not So Wonderful Copenhagen as some christened it after they left two weeks later with nothing but more fragments—extended fragments now, but fragments all the same.

Even Nigel Godrich was losing faith and he told them to "stop behaving like a bunch of fucking method actors." Thom was on a different page: "Nigel didn't understand why the fuck we'd want to do something else when we were so good at one thing." On April 12, they and their now sixty uncompleted songs fled to Batsford Park in Gloucestershire in the hope that another rural manor house would have the same effect as St Catherine's Court. They talked about splitting up. After all, if they couldn't finish anything, what was the point of going on?

"It wasn't just me who was reacting against *OK Computer*," argued Thom to *Mojo*. "Everyone was saying, 'We've got to start somewhere.' I'd go, 'Not there.' They'd reply, 'Well, where?' And I'd say, 'I don't know.' We'd launch ideas and I'd start screaming, 'This is bollocks, stop the tape' and start something else. Then we'd go back a few months later, listen to 'Morning Bell' and 'Like Spinning Plates' and think, 'That's fucking amazing, why did we stop?' We'd lost all confidence. We didn't have the ability to see anything through. As things gradually got back to normal, it became clear what was good and what wasn't."

With the band sessions in many shades of limbo, Ed co-wrote and contributed to some of Martin Phipps's soundtrack to the BBC mini-series of *Eureka Street*, Irish writer and band favorite Robert McLiam Wilson's novel of Catholic-Protestant friendships in Belfast. "It's a great book," Ed told *NME*. "I was completely blown away by it." Wilson's compliment was more oblique: "Radiohead's music cheers me up. I know it's not meant to, but it does."

Meeting People is Easy was launched in the United States in May, and Cait Selway gave birth to her first child, Leo. Then Thom and Jonny played a brief acoustic set at the 1999 Tibetan Freedom Concert in Amsterdam, alongside Garbage, Blue and, of course, Alanis Morissette. There was the brand new "Egyptian Song," a version of Elvis Costello's "I'll Wear It Proudly," and some crowd-pleasing *OK Computer* fare. Five days later, Thom could be found in Cologne attempting to present a Drop the Debt petition signed by seventeen million to the gathering G8 leaders. It demanded the cancellation of Third World debt. The pop star delegation (Thom, Bob Geldof, Bono, etc.) met German chancellor Gerhard Schröder, but when Thom joined the masses, riot police forced them through the cobbled backstreets where they were packed like sardines in a crushed tin box. He joined a human chain alongside the River Thames for the Jubilee 2000 movement. He even did some interviews for the project, but there was one taboo subject: "Radiohead are not relevant to this."

There was a return to Glastonbury, but this year Thom, Ed, and Nigel Godrich were simply backstage visitors. Ed was overheard to say nothing had been recorded for the new album.

By September they had agreed (a rarity in this period) that a fully revamped Canned Applause was the place to be after all. Now things began to gel and a release date of summer 2000 began to look possible. Everybody began to grasp the fact that there would not be a Motown or Stax or Smiths feel any more than there would be an *OK Computer* feel. Radiohead were going to rebuild themselves, more radically than they had ever rebuilt themselves. "If you're going to make a different record, you have to change the methodology," explained Ed to *Q*. "It's scary and everyone feels insecure, but it's a test. Honestly, honestly, honestly, everyone needs to know what it's like to have your toys taken away. We split the band. Then we reformed it with exactly the same members. There's no point carrying on as we were before. That's why we never look back and never talk about the past."

New ground rules were set: not every member would appear on every track; there would be no drums or guitars; and Jonny would fully master the ondes Martenot, arrange the strings and play recorder. He acquired a special digital ondes Martenot from a limited reproduction run of fifty, created by Maurice Martenot's son. Jonny's transcendent strings moment came when he summoned the Orchestra of St John's (who, significantly, were familiar with Krzysztof Penderecki) to Dorchester Abbey, a few miles south-east of their Abingdon base. Seeing Jonny as an innocent in the complex world of classical music, the orchestra weren't wholly impressed with his suggestion that they swung like jazz musicians, but an accord of sorts was reached.

Newly obsessed with volatile jazz pianist Bud Powell, Thom offered tone poems rather than lyrics, which, in a move to maximize creativity, would not be shown to his bandmates. On the album's release, there would be no singles, no videos, and very little press. No wonder it had taken them so long to dust themselves down. In fact, it's a wonder they made it to the starting line.

Luckily, they had an album title, "No Logo," after Canadian activist author Naomi Klein's best-selling polemic. The book discussed the ravages caused by brand-led corporatism and how to fight it. "It gave one real hope," noted Ed. "It certainly made me feel less alone. I must admit I am deeply pessimistic about humanity, but she was writing about everything I was trying to make sense of. It was very uplifting."

After being endorsed by one of the biggest brands in popular music, Naomi Klein began to receive letters from Radiohead fans, "asking how they could get involved in globalization activism. It made me realize how contagious optimism is."

Inspired by jazz giant Charles Mingus's boundary pushing 1960 album, *Blues & Roots*, Thom and Jonny recorded an eight-piece brass section, the Hook Horns, on what would become "The National Anthem" and told them to bring out their inner frustrated driver. Thom claimed to *Juice* magazine that he was so excited during the sessions that he jumped up and down and broke his foot. On December 19, Radiohead offered their first webcast, where "Knives Out" was premiered in not too dissimilar form to its finished version and the playlist would include Miles Davis, Squarepusher, Can, and Captain Beefheart. Before this strange year was out, Ed's Internet diary claimed that six songs had been completed. Just to remind them of the goodwill their about-turn was up against, *Spin* decided *OK Computer* was the ninth best album of the nineties (Nirvana's *Nevermind* won) and *Q* that Thom was the sixteenth most important star of the twentieth century (John Lennon won).

By Christmas they had six tracks completed, but the new century brought a new Radiohead. The recording sessions were grueling, but extraordinarily productive and the sense of despair evaporated. Even the skeptical slugabeds who had feared drastic change leapt on board. At Nigel Godrich's inspired suggestion, the band voluntarily split into two ever-rotating camps who beavered away, not on songs as such, but on samples, cut-ups, rhythms, and whatever sounded right, but didn't sound like *OK Computer*. There was no communication between the factions, just a circle of improvement and refinement. One team made sounds in the studio, another built on those sounds in the programming room without drums or guitars. The more they recorded, the more sense everything made. They weren't being drained by live dates and when Thom was happy with "The National Anthem," the dam burst. Phil had used cut-ups and samples on "Airbag," so he was keen to explore new territory, but his role as the band's musical conscience, the man with the final say on more takes than the average drummer, was never going to be usurped. Easy-going Colin ("I'd make a very good member of the royal family.") was a rhythm man to his core. Ed and Jonny were kids in the proverbial sweetshop, who relished discovering that the more chances they took, the better everything sounded. Following his muse and his instinct allowed Thom to cut the Gordian Knot of pressure that had almost enveloped him. As *Rolling Stone* would declare in a hysterical, but not wholly wide of the mark headline: "In Order to Save Themselves, Radiohead Had to Destroy Rock & Roll."

In March 2000, Thom recorded "I've Seen It All" with Björk for *Selmasongs: Music from the Motion Picture Soundtrack 'Dancer in the Dark'*. She inadvertently provided an epiphany for him when he heard her practice her scales early one morning. He'd already been to see a Harley Street specialist who'd taught him how to sing, from a medical point of view, but Björk's diligence flipped the switch. From now on, he'd take care of what he'd been given. "He is," Björk explained to *Time Out*, "a very pure soul. He doesn't do things lightly." By April, the making of the album was all over and, as Colin noted dryly to *NME*, "There was a lot of pain making it." The least fertile period in Radiohead history had turned into the most fertile: they had enough material for two albums. "I am," declared Jonny, "going for a walk in the park." Thom recorded "The Mess We're In," a duet with old chum and kindred spirit PJ Harvey for her gorgeous *Stories from the City, Stories from the Sea* album, on which he also added keyboards and backing vocals to "Beautiful Feeling" and "One Line." In time, he'd become obsessed with her 2007 album, *White Chalk*.

As a title, "No Logo" wasn't quite right, not least since Naomi Klein's opus was very much of its time. Kid A was a software program of children's voices which had long been cast aside from the final mix, but the ambiguity of the phrase appealed to Thom, suggesting both the first genetically cloned child ("I'm sure somewhere it's been done, even though it's illegal.") and the sense that Radiohead's artistic rebirth made them children once more. More than anything, though, it sounded right.

Once Jonny had returned from his walk in the park, the album was presented to EMI, whose US executives were forced to listen to the whole thing on a chartered bus between Hollywood and Malibu. The label had long been sanguine about the non-appearance of a follow-up to *OK Computer*, and all parties settled on a release date of October. Radiohead spent June and July touring some of Europe and Israel's more unusual venues, from Roman amphitheaters in Tel Aviv and Fréjus, south-east France, to the magnificent Piazza Santa Croce in central Florence, via the Villa Reale stately home in Monza, Italy. The surroundings suited the bedding in of new material such as "Dollars and Cents," "Morning Bell" and "Optimistic" which, at first listen, didn't especially seem made for the stage.

Parlophone got to work. That *Kid A* would not be an easy sell didn't mean it wouldn't sell. At one with their charges, the label understood the fan base was key. After all, this was the same fan base which had backed Radiohead's myriad changes and which the label now backed to proselytize the most seismic change of all. In league with the band, EMI drip-fed mini-movies set to *Kid A* music to assorted websites, bypassing traditional print media, MTV, and radio. Back then, few believed the Internet had the power to make or break albums and no globally successful act had attempted such an audacious move. Three weeks before its release, *Kid A* was "leaked" to the peer-to-peer file sharing service Napster, from which, briefly, potential purchasers could stream the album for free.

Simultaneously, with no serious promotion to do, the band embarked upon the *No Logo* tour. Deliberately avoiding the festival circuit this time, like fairground carneys, these traveling minstrels played in a tent. Not just any old tent, of course, but an acoustically optimized, ten thousand-capacity, unsponsored, advertisement-free Kayam tent.

As Jonny noted in an interview for the tent manufacturers, it was about having total control of their self-created environment. "It's been frustrating when we've arrived at venues and there's been adverts on beer cups etc. Being in control means you can do what you want. The sound in the tent is much better than the sound in an arena."

The new logistics and a movable venue meant new places to play: parks in Britain, racecourses in Ireland, a soccer field in wonderful-again Copenhagen. Twinkly lights gave the tent the look and feel of a magical castle, inside which something special would happen. By the time *Kid A* was formally released on October 2, 2000, there was an understanding of what people would—and wouldn't—be getting.

Nigel Godrich had a new credit, "recording directed by." Thom had a new nom-de-design for his work with Stanley Donwood, Tchock (probably derived from Chocky, the titular alien in John Wyndham's 1968 novel), a nightmare scenario described as "landscapes, knives and glue" on the sleeve. Was there a portrait of Tony Blair embedded in its pages?

Frankly, it's hard to tell for sure, but Thom was true to his intention to explain nothing. There were lyrics included, but they weren't the correct lyrics. Instead, Stanley Donwood and Tchock designed a weighty booklet, layout similar to a Victorian circus flyer, packed with lyrics from *Kid A* and elsewhere ("with a grin like roadkill" came from "Ed's Scary Song," Ed's never-released melodrama). It looked like a peek into torment.

The music, though, was in many senses, something else. Despite Thom's professed aversion, there were melodies—melodies to spare in fact—but they were buried under the avalanche of innovation. For the first eight seconds of the opening "Everything in Its Right Place," when Jonny's lovely, melodic piano promised a sweet song of rue and wonder, it seemed as though those rumors of radical transformation were overdramatic. Then, something else piped up: a discordant hum that sounded as if it was recorded through a snorkel, before two Thoms joined in, one crooning, the other muttering, both more instrument than adornment. The song glided forth for four more minutes. Its right place turned out to be the opening sequence of Cameron Crowe's *Vanilla Sky*, where Tom Cruise (Tom Cruise!) wanders around New York as if everything is going to work out just fine . . .

Written on Thom's home baby grand piano, lyrically it revisited the aftermath of the troubled Birmingham NEC show of 1997. "I came off, sat in the dressing room and I actually couldn't speak," he told *Rolling Stone*. "People were saying, 'You all right?' I knew people were speaking to me. But I couldn't hear them. I'd just so had enough. And I was bored with saying I'd had enough. I was beyond that. Lots of people say the song is gibberish, but it's not, it's about that. I love it."

Having failed to materialize properly in Paris and Copenhagen, it was the first completed *Kid A* song and, alongside "The National Anthem," it prised Thom from his writer's block. "It wasn't really a writer's block," he told *Mojo*. "In fact, words were coming out like diarrhea, but they were

KID A

RECORDED AT Guillaume Tell, Paris; Medley, Copenhagen; Unnamed studio, Oxfordshire

PRODUCED BY Nigel Godrich & Radiohead

PERSONNEL
Colin Greenwood
Ed O'Brien
Jonny Greenwood
Phil Selway
Thom Yorke

ADDITIONAL PERSONNEL
Orchestra of St John's: strings
Hook Horns: horns on "The National Anthem"

COVER ART
Stanley: artwork ("Landscapes, Knives and Glue")
Tchock: artwork ("Landscapes, Knives and Glue")

RELEASED Oct 2, 2000

LABEL Parlophone, CDKIDA 1

HIGHEST CHART POSITION ON RELEASE UK 1, US 1, FRA 1, NL 4, NZ 1, SWE 3, CAN 1, SWI 8, AUS 2, ITA 3

TRACK LIST
Everything in Its Right Place
Kid A
The National Anthem
How to Disappear Completely
Treefingers
Optimistic
In Limbo
Idioteque
Morning Bell
Motion Picture Soundtrack
(song ends at 3:17; includes an untitled hidden track from 4:17 until 5:12, followed by 1:44 of silence)

NOTES
"Idioteque" contains two samples from the Odyssey title First Recordings – Electronic Music Winners (1976): Paul Lansky's "Mild und Leise" and Arthur Kreiger's "Short Piece".

"That Kid A would not be an easy sell, didn't meant it wouldn't sell."

all awful. I couldn't tell, which was much worse because I'd lost all confidence." It was a maelstrom of ideas: Autechre-style cut-ups, a hint of the *Doctor Who* theme, the piano programmed into a laptop and Radiohead's old friends: threat, beauty, and, when Thom panders to preconception by singing of waking up sucking a lemon, mischief. There's always mischief with Radiohead—it explains more than any heart-of-darkness, tortured-Thom theory. "Actually, waking up sucking a lemon was the face I had for three years," chortled Thom.

The title track was the sound of a clenched fist. Ed's Moog was all over it and he explained to Q the sense of liberation the new way of doing things had given him. The penny had well and truly dropped. "You find yourself operating machines you've never used before and you're like a kid. It's so fantastic to realize it's as valid as a really great guitar riff." Once more overturning the notion that acoustic = authentic, there were cut-ups everywhere, drum samples to spare, Jonny's covert melody, gentle nods towards Warp's Boards of Canada (the elusive Scottish brothers who specialized in mournful sampling), and Thom's hideously distorted (through a vocoder via Jonny's ondes Martenot) vocals. It was made more sinister still by the Pied Piper lyrical imagery and suggestions of Werner Herzog's demented but wonderful *Nosferatu the Vampyre*. Thom claimed he plucked the lyrics from a top hat, part William Burroughs, part fridge magnet aficionado. The miasma of abduction and foul play is everywhere. This is music as fog.

Extreme, beguiling, and formerly titled "Everyone," Thom's favorite track, "The National Anthem," begins with him playing a bass riff from the On A Friday days so relentless it could underpin a Warp track, a Red Hot Chili Peppers swaggerthon, or a seventies disco tune with equal assuredness.

The very title shows how careful Radiohead are with words. Outside Anfield, the ground of Liverpool FC, one of England's leading soccer teams, there's a 1997 statue of Bill Shankly, who managed them to unprecedented triumphs in the sixties and seventies. Born of mining stock, Shankly never lost his rough edges and his connection with the beleaguered residents of the dilapidated port that was Liverpool, even as The Beatles rose. Tom Murphy's statue is a beauty, showing Shankly in crumpled suit, Liverpool FC scarf around his neck, arms aloft. Its inscription is just as beautiful: "He made the people happy." It's the word "the" that makes it right. Similarly, "National Anthem" is one thing, but "The National Anthem" is another, infinitely superior, beast.

It's another royal mess and, according to Phil, it was scrapped on the grounds of sounding too much like indie also-rans Kitchens of Distinction during rehearsals for *The Bends*. On *Kid A*, it never fails to add something new with each listen. The guitar lays the foundation for a swirling maelstrom of excess. Jonny's ondes Martenot adds spook, but there's the Hook Horns' brass aiming scattergun sniper fire, which is surely what Thom envisaged when he'd heard Charles Mingus and encouraged the eight blowers to play like drivers stuck in traffic. Jonny's appreciation of Karlheinz Stockhausen and John Cage added a further veneer of complexity and, somewhere in there, Thom is crooning more sweetly than ever.

After that, "How to Disappear Completely" feels like a comedown. When it was played in front of Nigel Godrich during the *OK Computer* tour, it had already endured a long, difficult gestation. Its line "I float down the Liffey" came from Thom's unhappy out-of-body experience at the Dublin RDS show (another of his lowest era's traumas revisited on *Kid A*) and, beyond Doug Richmond's book, the inspiration came from Michael Stipe's advice on dealing with panic attacks, which involved disappearing completely, mentally at least, when pressure really bore down. At various points lasting seven, ten, and fourteen minutes, before the *Kid A* version settled on six, it was a great idea nobody knew quite how to execute, until Thom walked away, allowing Jonny to add some Dorchester Abbey strings. And a tambourine.

Thom fashioned "Treefingers" from some of Ed's stray chords, but it was really Jonny's *Kid A* peak. It merged his love of sixties organist Jimmy Smith with the snail's pace grandeur of Vangelis's *Blade Runner* soundtrack, Brian Eno-esque atmospherics, their old teachers Can, and Ed's wibbling guitar. There are no words, but there is a spirit of optimism and renewal that wouldn't have seen it out of place on a BBC nature documentary. Radiohead albums tend to have a moment of calm and a clearly defined halfway point where the narrative arc begins to descend. This was *Kid A*'s, although Radiohead being Radiohead they neglected to play it live until 2012 and then only twice.

If "Treefingers" was optimistic, "Optimistic" most certainly wasn't, but it was to *Kid A* what "Electioneering" was to *OK Computer*. On a musical level, despite a jumping ending wholly out of kilter with what precedes it, its conventional structure and instrumentation make it the least adventurous branch on the *Kid A* tree. Yet, it fits perfectly between "Treefingers" and "In Limbo" and it jump-starts the second half. Colin referred to it as the "Phil is Don Henley" song and, for once, Phil drums like a rocker. Thom's seemingly undoctored vocals are more upfront than at any point since *The Bends*; the guitarwork is back in Magazine territory; it almost has a chorus and, much to Thom's chagrin, on an album without singles, "Optimistic" was selected by too many radio planners as airplay material. Not wholly coincidentally, it's also *Kid A*'s most overtly political moment. It's as if, in order to get his point over, Thom decided he must be clear. The others fell out of love with it long before Thom.

Lyrically, it's informed by the broad thrusts of Naomi Klein's *No Logo*, but the line "the best you can is good enough" was balm offered to Thom by Rachel Owen. Thom's claim that he saw dinosaurs rampaging over the planet whenever he sang it makes some sense. But not much.

Originally titled "Lost at Sea" and written about writer's block (one surefire way out of writer's block is to write about it), being rootless, and the Dante's *Inferno* audiotape Rachel Owen played in the car as she studied for her PhD at Royal Holloway, University of London, "In Limbo" is a return to *Kid A*'s core values and to Thom's winning way with a croon. They'd first attempted a version at a New York soundcheck in 1998, but it was soon forgotten. Desperate for any kind of inspiration, they revisited it at Guillaume Tell, where they added layers of found sound and the claustrophobic, hemmed-in feel Thom sought. Unusually, Thom was the first to be happy, but the others pushed on and the result hurtles along, building towards urgency as the ondes Martenot pulls its weight, while ghostly samples add menace and when it climaxes with an almighty whoosh, the deal is sealed. Thom claimed it sounded like The Police, but he may very well have been joking.

A chunk of an hour-long collage, "Idioteque" distills all that was great about Radiohead in this period. These are shifting sands, but it's probably *Kid A*'s high point and lest we forget, its chorus is irresistible. The samples were obscure but credited after being discovered by Jonny on the 1976 compilation *First Recordings – Electric Music Winners*: a four-chord sequence from *Mild und Leise*, a lengthy 1972 computer-based opus by American composer Paul Lansky, and Arthur Kreiger's appositely titled *Short Piece*. The two composers had become professors and both obscure toilers would soon enjoy a Radiohead-sized royalty cheque: Paul Lansky even came to see a Radiohead show in New York. This was compromise-free: no guitar, no bass, no drums, no keyboards, just Jonny's ondes Martenot, those samples, and a host of electronica. "For me," Ed wryly noted to *Q*, "it was about being a participant without playing a note."

Kid A is not a simple album, but "Morning Bell" is its simplest moment. Naturally, this means that recording it was unspeakably complicated and when radically revised versions appeared on two subsequent albums (although the *Amnesiac* version pre-dates the *Kid A* one) it was clear Radiohead were far from sure how to proceed. The *Kid A* version is sad and smooth with a soupcon of jazzy bossa nova propping up Thom's growl-free vocals. Phil's drumming emulates Charlie Watts's always-appropriate simplicity; Jonny's ominous keyboards (he plays guitar too) drench the whole tune in dread, and when Thom starts muttering at the end, it's a death rattle. Just as The Human League's "Louise" is an update on the couple in "Don't You Want Me," "Morning Bell" returned us to the squabbling pair, violent undercurrent and all, of "No Surprises" and "Black Star." This time, though, it's about the children and when Thom suggests cutting the kids in half, it's as wise as Solomon, but the prospect that such whimsy is meant to be taken literally cannot be entirely discounted.

Radiohead always did know how to close an album, even *Pablo Honey*. "Motion Picture Soundtrack" had been knocking around since the "Creep" era like some Word Update that wouldn't take and John Leckie had been keen for it to make *The Bends*. Originally, the wine in the first line was white rather than red and it had a full second half. Here, after a gap of sixty-three seconds, it has a fifty-second coda, a "A Day in the Life"-esque sustained note with a snatch of choir (a Jonny sample) which bears little relation to the first half. Then, seemingly apropos of nothing, there is a further fifty-one seconds of silence.

It's a peculiar concoction, although not wholly mis-titled. Thom thought it sounded like "Zip-a-Dee-Doo-Dah," which is wide of the mark, but the sweeping harp (another Jonny sample) and the unashamed sense of wonder do give it something of a Disney incidental music feel, albeit Disney channeled through Alice Coltrane. Jonny's wheezy harmonium could have backed Tom Waits on "Hang Down Your Head" or propelled a Salvation Army recruiting drive, while Thom is at his most sinisterly detached. It sounds like the heralding of an interval rather than an ending. So it would prove.

What the hell had happened? *OK Computer* had succeeded via its own brilliance and the Stakhanovite work ethic that so nearly derailed Thom. But this? This utter rejection of their own greatness, their very own *Neither Fish nor Flesh* on the heels of *Introducing the Hardline According to Terence Trent D'Arby*? Reviewers were baffled, but *NME*'s Keith Cameron perceptively noted that the Aphex Twin undercurrent was "significant only because we know (and they know we know) that it's been made by a multi-million unit-shifting rock band." Less perceptively, the phrase "commercial suicide" was bandied around with overly gay abandon by a smorgasbord of reviewers who really should have known better.

But, but, but . . . The dust didn't take that long to settle. Thom may have wished "Optimistic" had not been singled out for airplay, but it was a gateway and moreover it was a gateway into an extraordinary record, one which would beguile, enlighten, and provide additional moments of wonder every time it was played. It bears repeating that Radiohead have never wanted to be unsuccessful: they made *Kid A* to consolidate their success, but on their own terms. They wanted to create the conditions which would keep them alive as a group and they worked so hard at creating those conditions that it almost finished them. Whatever the opposite of "commercial suicide" is, *Kid A* is that. It was made to succeed, not to fail, not to downscale. As Thom observed: "If *Kid A* is difficult, then there really is no fucking hope for us."

That said, it was brave, almost to the point of self-delusion. *OK Computer* was hardly Backstreet Boys, but *Kid A* was something else: It was weird, it was difficult despite Thom's claims and to enter its cavern of jewels, hurdles had to be overcome. Good.

There would be no real publicity, so the fan base was left to assert itself. Every Radiohead album involved a leap of faith. This time, the leap of faith had just gotten a whole lot bigger, but the principle was identical. The airing of some of the songs live and EMI's drip-feeding prior to *Kid*

A's release had diminished the unknown factor. Soon, Radiohead's best, most faithful friend, "word of mouth," worked its magic. Extraordinarily, *Kid A* reached No. 1 in the British and American charts, surely the most left-field album to do the double. In the UK nothing quite so "difficult" since Leftfield's *Rhythm and Stealth*, and in the US since Rage Against The Machine's *The Battle of Los Angeles*, had been grasped to the public's bosom so enthusiastically that it topped the album charts. Radiohead had won much more than the Grammy *Kid A* would be given in 2000 for Best Alternative Music Album, even if band and album weren't the alternative to anything.

Ed later told *Q* he took magic mushrooms to make that Grammy ceremony more interesting: "You're supposed to say it's really false, but I had a fucking great evening." He had started to meditate: "It's the most profound thing you can do," the batsman and cricket obsessive told *Wisden Cricket Monthly* in 2018. "It helped me when I was at my lowest ebb. I do it every day for 20 minutes."

There were new fans too. Those who had found *OK Computer* too prog, too overbearing, and too angsty would find as much to love in *Kid A* as those Radiohead devotees still thrilled to be along for the remarkable ride. Weeks after *Kid A*'s release, a triumphant appearance on *Saturday Night Live* was stakes-raising evidence that "The National Anthem" and "Idioteque" soared still higher in front of a national television audience.

Questions remained. Those initial song fragments had been whittled down and worked up into enough material for a double album, but neither band—Phil in particular—nor label were in favor of swamping purchasers with two hours of newness. There hadn't been quite the agonizing over running order which had nearly delayed *OK Computer*, but there was much more debate about which songs merited inclusion. As ever—the omission of "Lift" from *OK Computer* still rankled with some—those which made the cut weren't necessarily the best songs, just the ones which sounded right. The bigger picture trumps all, but what were they to do with all that unused material? Taking ten songs for *Kid A* meant there were still thirteen to play with.

Still wary of how close they had come to disintegrating during the *OK Computer* whirl and then during the making of *Kid A*, Radiohead needed yet another new approach, ideally one which didn't involve them touring to fill any inspiration gaps. The solution was right there in front of them. If it was indeed true that the tracks which comprised *Kid A* weren't selected on merit alone (it was; they weren't); if it was true that what remained would make a coherent album (it was; it would); and if they could cope with shuffling rather than hurtling forwards (they could, but only just), they had another, wholly legitimate album ready to go, without the heartache of actually making it. Colin skeptically confessed that "I'm not sure they are two records," but the collective will triumphed, and before the year was out they confirmed it on their website. Once the American tour finished in October 2000 in Los Angeles, Jonny promised a New York radio station that the fifth Radiohead album would be ready for April 2001. They set to work selecting and sequencing.

It took longer, of course (but only until June), not least since Thom and Rachel Owen's son, Noah, was born in February ("Kids teach you to lighten up, which for me was very handy because I wasn't very light at the time," Thom mused. "He spends a lot of time talking to the fairies.") but the gap between albums was still just eight months. In April, Ed and Phil found themselves in Auckland, New Zealand playing five shows at the St James Theatre alongside Pearl Jam's Eddie Vedder and The Smiths' Johnny Marr in Neil Finn's 7 Worlds Collide band, covering songs from Neil Finn's catalog, Pearl Jam, and The Smiths, but not Radiohead. The pair enjoyed the experience so much they would repeat it in 2009 on *The Sun Came Out*, the studio-based follow-up in aid of Oxfam, where

Ed co-wrote "Learn to Crawl" with Johnny Marr, Neil Finn and son Liam Finn. Phil's "The Ties That Bind Us" was covered too.

Craftily, *Amnesiac* was pitched as similar yet noticeably different to *Kid A*. "It's about the things you forget. And remembering," Thom half-explained to *The Big Issue*, before telling *Q* it was "the sound of what it feels like to be standing in the fire." They were being slightly but not wholly disingenuous: *Kid A* had one mood, while *Amnesiac* would have another. "Some tracks on *Amnesiac* are harder to get into than most on *Kid A*," explained Jonny. "It's distributed that way on purpose, but there are possibly more straight-ahead songs on *Amnesiac*. Maybe that makes it easier to listen to in the end."

There was brass on a Radiohead album for the second time in a row (but with very different participants to those on "The National Anthem") and Thom promised it would be "back to the guitar," although in fairness he also promised, "We are definitely having singles, videos and glossy magazine photoshoots. There will be children's television appearances, dance routines and many interesting interviews about my tortured existence." Colin suggested the album would be "more conventional but more dissonant," which may or may not have been correct. What teasers they had become.

Either way, in May 2001, "Pyramid Song," Radiohead's first British single in three years, swept to No. 5. First played at the 1999 Tibetan Freedom Concert with Thom on piano, when it was titled "Nothing to Fear," it was resurrected as "Egyptian Song" at Meltdown in London in 2000. Thom was at the height of his Charles Mingus phase, especially the handclap-laden "Freedom," so there were handclaps all over it, until the band realized how ghastly they sounded. What remained on the re-retitled (at Jonny's insistence) "Pyramid Song" was a near-flamenco strum that began as a rare jam, this time between Thom and Phil, whose drums crash in after two minutes. There are Igor Stravinsky-style strings,

AMNESIAC

RECORDED AT Dorchester Abbey, Oxfordshire

PRODUCED BY Nigel Godrich & Radiohead

PERSONNEL
Colin Greenwood
Ed O'Brien
Jonny Greenwood
Phil Selway
Thom Yorke

ADDITIONAL PERSONNEL
Orchestra of St John's: strings on "Pyramid Song" and "Dollars and Cents"
Band on "Life in a Glasshouse"
Humphrey Lyttelton: trumpet, bandleader
Jimmy Hastings: clarinet
Pete Strange: trombone
Paul Bridge: double bass
Adrian Macintosh: drums

COVER ART
Stanley Donwood: pictures, design
Tchocky: pictures

RELEASED Jun 5, 2001

LABEL Parlophone, CDFHEIT 45101

HIGHEST CHART POSITION ON RELEASE UK 1, US 2, FRA 2, NZ 1, CAN 1, SWI 6, AUS 2, ITA 2, GER 2

TRACK LIST
Packt Like Sardines in a Crushd Tin Box
Pyramid Song
Pulk/Pull Revolving Doors
You and Whose Army?
I Might Be Wrong
Knives Out
Morning Bell/Amnesiac
Dollars and Cents
Hunting Bears
Like Spinning Plates
Life in a Glasshouse

"[Amnesiac is] the sound of what it feels like to be standing in the fire." THOM

an unusually high level of soul, and a lyric which, if squinted at from a certain angle, had something of "Swing Low, Sweet Chariot" about it, although Thom had been reading husband and wife Graham Hancock and Santha Faiia's cod-historical *Heaven's Mirror: Quest for the Lost Civilization*. It was another mess, yet another glorious mess which worked when it really shouldn't.

Despite *Amnesiac*'s muted quest for difference, there were almost no surprises. Having come to terms with one *Kid A*, a year later, most purchasers were more than keen to hear the same yet different. *Amnesiac* sailed to No. 1 in Britain and 2 in the US, empirical proof that people liked *Kid A* so much they wanted Kid B. Nigel Godrich had a deserved new, simplified credit, "produced by"; Thom had a new art pseudonym, Tchocky—*Amnesiac* would win a Grammy for Best Recording Package—and just to make sure there was no sleight of hand, it was noted on the sleeve that "These recordings were made on location at the same time as *Kid A*."

It began with what sounded like Phil clanging some pots and pans, the sort of cacophony IRA sympathizers used to warn when a British army raid was imminent. "Packt Like Sardines in a Crushd Tin Box," was a subtle opener. Beyond Thom demanding to be left alone—"I'm a reasonable man, get off my case"—all emotion was sucked out of him by the Auto-Tune voice processor which had added icy charm to Cher's "Believe" and which Thom used for effect rather than inability to carry a tune. The percussion propels it; the farmyard growls add atmosphere; the lyrics came to Thom while people-watching at Paris's Place des Vosges; and the collapsed section towards the end suggests that Bollywood could be Radiohead's for the taking. Does it sound like *Kid A*? A little. Would it have fitted on *Kid A*? Absolutely not. Why, it's almost as if they knew what they were doing.

Colin's favorite *Amnesiac* track, the loop-heavy "Pulk/Pull Revolving Doors" had Thom on Auto-Tune for the second and final time. Here, it turned him into an infant Dalek who'd just read *Alice in Wonderland*. What went on behind him, though, was another leap into the unknown. These are some of Radiohead's most fierce, most uncompromising backbeats—the Warp sound, but pushed harder still, almost to distortion, with brief moments of tension-lowering twinkle. It's brutal.

He wasn't to know in 2001, but Thom's distrust of Tony Blair and George W. Bush would come to seem rather petty. Back then, nobody could have predicted what was to follow, so his complaints resonated and "You and Whose Army?" was his most overtly political moment outside his activism. "It's about someone who's elected into power," he told *Mojo*, tellingly going into metaphor-free detail. "And then he blatantly betrays them, just like Blair did. The man's a fool: a court jester."

Looking for a swinging feel close to The Ink Spots, the great New York vocal group of the forties and fifties, they attempted to record it with instruments of the era, but that proved unworkable, so Jonny's ondes Martenot faked the backing vocals before they were doctored in the studio. While recording *Kid A* and *Amnesiac*, Thom had devoured *Revolution in the Head*, Ian MacDonald's definitive guide to Beatles recording sessions. Now he tried to emulate them by singing "You and Whose Army?" through an egg-box, not that anybody would notice in the end. It's not their finest moment. The band who specialize in being of no place and time were undone by a lyric which quickly dated and the rare feeling that they might have spent more time on their creation.

After such density, "I Might Be Wrong" is the lightest moment of the whole period. The choppy guitars chime and hurry along with a spring in their jaunty step. Colin was channeling his inner Bernard Edwards; Phil's drums are distinctly two-step; and Thom's first-take vocals are unusually airy, perhaps because he had taken inspiration from Rachel Owen's demand that he "let the bad stuff go." He ignored her, until he didn't: "One day you finally hear and, after months and months of utter fucking torment, you finally understand," and so it's a song of rebirth. Naturally, being conventional for a whole song was a step too far and four minutes in, apropos of nothing, it collapses into a Beach Boys-esque coda of loveliness.

If "I Might Be Wrong" flirted with convention, "Knives Out," the song from the first webcast back in December 1999, embraced it. This might have been what Ed was thinking of when he thought *Kid A/Amnesiac* was going to be a catchy, Smithsian affair where the group would "get rid of all the effects, have really nice sounding guitars and do something snappy." Indeed, he played an early version to Smiths guitarist Johnny Marr. "He explained they'd tried to take a snapshot of how I'd done things in The Smiths. It was an unbelievable experience. I was beyond flattered," Johnny Marr remembered in 2004. More dominant than they had been since *The Bends*, the flamenco-tinged guitars were at the front of the mix and, as they detailed another collapsing suburban relationship, Thom's vocals were baggage-free. It all sounds very straightforward, but, as we know, being simple can be complicated, especially if you're Radiohead, so it took them 373 days to finish. "By the end, I really hated that song," shrugged Thom to *Mojo*. Many months after eulogizing it to Johnny Marr, Ed concurred in the Tel Aviv newspaper *Ha'ir*, "I got bored: it took too long to get it done."

Putting a *Kid A* song on *Amnesiac* when "Worry Wort" and "Kinetic" would not make either was an audacious move and since the *Amnesiac* version was recorded first, surely a planned one. If "Morning Bell" was *Kid A*'s most bossa nova moment, on *Amnesiac* (which ironically had more actual bossa nova) it was more angular and with atmospherics worthy of John Carpenter, much more filmic. With slightly altered lyrics, it worked perfectly on *Amnesiac*, just as the other version worked perfectly on *Kid A*.

The Can-style, eleven-minute improvised version of "Dollars and Cents" they flirted with in the Copenhagen sessions was always a work in progress. The elbows-sharpened version on *Amnesiac* fought the flab and retained a mood so anxious it could have slotted into *OK Computer*. Thom has had less studenty lyrics than this quixotic notion of small change unseating big business, but when his muttering is pitched against his soaring backing vocals, you'd forgive him anything.

The slender, two-minutes-long instrumental "Hunting Bears" occurs too late to be an interval, but it is a pause for thought, if only to wonder how it links with the recurring artwork motif of bears which, Thom told *Blender*, "stemmed initially from a deep paranoia of genetic engineering." Quite. Thom's keyboards rage gently against Jonny's distorted guitars, the closest he's come to Ry Cooder-style wizardry.

Showing once again he is not as other men, when Thom heard the melody to "I Will," which would resurface, much changed, on *Hail to the Thief*, his first thought was to wonder what it might sound like backwards. "I heard it backwards and thought, 'ah ha, that's the right way,'" he told *Wire*, as if nothing could be more obvious. Everyone else agreed and "Like Spinning Plates" is perhaps the one song on *Amnesiac* that might have been better placed on *Kid A*. As Jonny expanded to Italian magazine *Mondo Sonoro*, "It's an incredibly emotional song, but not an easy one to grasp." It's Radiohead at their most out-there, and Thom's distorted, backwards vocals enhance the dislocated but threatening feel, before Colin adds Rhodes piano. "In terms of trying to get to something new, it's the best on the record," gushed Thom. "When I listen to it in the car, it makes the doors shake."

"Life in a Glasshouse" isn't just *Amnesiac*'s finale, it's the end of the whole *Kid A/Amnesiac* project, the end of Radiohead's response to *OK Computer*. Finally accepting they couldn't play jazz, they recruited the real thing: the four-strong brass section (plus extra drummer, Adrian Macintosh), led by the mighty trumpeter, cartoonist, calligrapher, and humorist, Humphrey Lyttelton, who died in 2008 aged eighty-six having turned down a knighthood. On Lyttelton's death, Jonny reflected: "He was an inspiring person to record with and without his direction, we'd never have recorded/released 'Life in a Glasshouse.' Go find 'Bad Penny Blues' and celebrate his life with some hot jazz."

As Lyttelton refused to communicate by telephone, Jonny had written to the man universally known as "Humph" admitting, "It's probably an awful cheek and we know you're very busy, but we're a bit stuck."

Being in his late seventies, Lyttelton was unfamiliar with Radiohead, but his daughter wasn't. Lyttelton and band met Greenwood and band in a Bayswater studio in West London for a seven-hour session.

"They didn't want it to sound like a slick studio production but a slightly exploratory thing," Lyttelton told Q. "However, I detected some sort of eye-rolling at the start of the session, as if to say we were miles apart. They went through quite a few nervous breakdowns just explaining it to us. My chops were getting in a very ragged state, so when we finally got a take that sounded good to me, they said, 'Good, we'll have some food, then we'll come back and do some more.' I said, 'Not me.' It was a very heavy day." Radiohead and Lyttelton's ensemble reunited for the song's only live airing during the Radiohead special on the BBC's *Later with Jools Holland* in June 2001.

Lyttelton and his men added a mournful, downbeat, New Orleans-funeral feel, to a mournful downbeat idea that had been in gestation since the *OK Computer* period. It was loosely based on an unnamed famous actor's wife who, Thom believed, when confronted by a baying pack of photographers, put up tabloid images of her so they were photographing themselves. As Thom told *Wire*, it was about having to compromise too: "If you're interested in being heard, you have to work within the system." If "Motion Picture Soundtrack" was an interval, "Life in a Glasshouse" was unquestionably a full stop.

Amnesiac isn't the greatest moment of Radiohead's career, but it's not short of great moments (Phil always regarded it as superior to *Kid A*) and not releasing *Kid A* as a double album was a masterstroke. Being a companion to *Kid A*, *Amnesiac* necessarily couldn't be a leap forward, although "Pulk/Pull Revolving Doors" clearly was. Its real triumph though was that it gave Radiohead the space to be a different kind of Radiohead. At one stroke, they'd bought time and taken themselves off the treadmill. For all the deleterious effect on his life, even Thom had come around to the view that promoting *OK Computer* so heavily was the right course of action at the time, but that doesn't mean he would do it again. *Kid A* and *Amnesiac* meant he wouldn't have to.

Thom: return of the mack.

8
ROAMING IN THE GLOAMING

They were not idle, though. Less than a month after *Amnesiac's* June 2001 release, Radiohead were back in the USA and Canada, starting the tour at The Woodlands, a planned Texan community from which the Butler brothers had recently fled to form Arcade Fire. The days of endless treks across middle America were over, but even here, they bisected the tour with a glorious homecoming they seemed uncharacteristically desperate to have. On July 7, overcoming local council objections by paying a £25,000 venue hire fee and donating all profits to charity, they played Oxford's 42,000-capacity South Park, where Keith Wozencroft had first seen On A Friday all those years ago. "At 11pm on the evening before the concert, I climbed onto the stage and looked across the empty park while the lighting designer rehearsed the light sequences. It was magical, like watching a private fireworks display," remembered Colin years later. "I was living in Southfield Road at the time and I could walk from my front door to the stage in five minutes."

These events tend to promise more than they deliver and just as no man is a hero in his own home, no internationally successful band are heroes in their own town. That it rained and that Thom was in taciturn mood didn't help, but afterwards he admitted to Molly McGrann that he'd wept towards the end. Over two-and-a-half hours they played twenty-four songs including, for the first time since the 1998 Tibetan Freedom Concert, "Creep." None of the 24 were un-released.

In August 2001, the single "Knives Out" reached No. 13 in the UK; the following month *Q* once again voted *OK Computer* the best album of all time (*Kid A* was thirteenth) and, in October, a little world tour featuring dates in Northern Ireland, Germany, Norway, Sweden, and five in Japan ended in Yokohama.

It was time for the "What Now?" question once again, but once again (and for the very last time) the response would be almost instant. November 12 saw the release of *I Might Be Wrong: Live Recordings*, five months after *Amnesiac* and thirteen after *Kid A*. Not just any live album, this was a Radiohead live album. The timing may have been odd, as two albums in five months was hardly mystique-building for increasingly exposure-shy megastars, but maybe the question shouldn't have been "Why?" but "Why not?"

Since *The Bends*, Radiohead had used the stage as a playpen, introducing new songs, sometimes years ahead of their recorded versions, before building them in public, changing title, lyrics, and instrumentation in the quest for something that sounded right. Why not, indeed?

This wasn't a history lesson, since the four dates from which the songs were culled were all from 2001, but it was more confirmation of Thom's notion that "The ideal mental state for me to perform live is when it feels as if I'm driving through the night." Seven of the eight songs were taken from *Kid A* or *Amnesiac*, while the long-labored-over "True Love Waits" had never appeared on an album at all. "We could make it sound like John Meyer," said Thom cryptically, "but nobody wants to do that."

These takes bore only passing resemblance to the still-new album versions, and if this was a case of playing to the gallery with its "Ooh, look at us, constantly evolving" approach, this is who Radiohead are. Like some bad-tempered sharks, Radiohead cannot stay still or they will die.

"The National Anthem" and "Everything in Its Right Place" came from a show in Vaison-la-Romaine in south-east France. The horn-free former was a showcase for Colin, then at the height of his Donald "Duck" Dunn—the great Stax bassist—phase, while the Autechre cut-ups had been downgraded in favor of something altogether more groovy. Jonny's ondes Martenot worked its magic and Thom's vocals were breathtaking. At seven minutes, the latter was the longest song on what the band pretended was an EP even when it reached No. 23 in the UK album charts and 44 in the US. "A Too Short Album" might have been a more apposite description. Any audience participation was almost extinguished.

The Oxford extravaganza provided "I Might Be Wrong," "Morning Bell," "Idioteque" and "Dollars and Cents," and they were all revamped. With the keyboards downplayed, "I Might Be Wrong" was now a beast from a nearby swamp, while "Morning Bell" bravely nodded to Supertramp and Ed's backing vocals were Vegas-period Elvis Presley. "Idioteque" had more strumming and less electronics, and a dubby "Dollars and Cents" repeatedly threatened to burst into ska.

"Like Spinning Plates" was the only track to hail from America, Jim Jarmusch's home, Cuyahoga Falls, Ohio, in fact. Thom adored the juddering recorded version, but here on the album's most radical revision, it's simpler, more emotional, and its keyboards are as affecting as anything on a Michael Nyman soundtrack.

Finally, from Oslo, the previously unreleased "True Love Waits." It wasn't new at all. It had been played in Brussels by Thom and Jonny as long ago as 1995 in acoustic form and it saw an unusually romantic Thom ruminating over the passage of time. It had been mooted for *OK Computer*, but it missed the cut, as it did for *Kid A*, despite returning to the set in Tel Aviv in 2000, and it almost made *Amnesiac*. "It's a great song," Ed argued in his Internet diary. "It's simply trying to find a way of doing it that excites us." They would find that later, but for the live album, it returned to its acoustic roots and Thom strummed it solo. "We tried to record it countless times, but it never worked," Nigel Godrich told *Rolling Stone* in 2012. "The irony is that you have the shitty live version."

NME preferred the live versions to the studio ones and suggested *I Might Be Wrong: Live Recordings* was their alive album, rather than merely their live one, and it proved once and for all that there is no "right" version of a Radiohead song, only different ones. Its brevity meant it would always be a case of what might have been, and there was something craven in looking back, but not looking back very far. It's an adjunct, but as *Q* intriguingly suggested, "It might prove more durable than its parents."

Naturally, there were no live dates in support of the live album. Colin played on "Blowback," "Fortress Europe" and the title track of the ever-angry Asian Dub Foundation's *Enemy of the Enemy* album, and having given up his photography hobby, Jonny (helped by Colin) took time to record an eighty-minute, string-laden, instrumental soundtrack to the art documentary *Bodysong*. It was released in October 2003, with a sleeve design by Jonny's wife, Sharona Katan. It was viewed by, amongst others, Paul Thomas Anderson, soon to loom large in Radiohead's world. "Jonny always wanted to mess with expectations," said director Simon Pummell. "At one point he was looking into soundscapes of extinct languages."

There was a familiar plan, though: write new material; rehearse it; tour it; record it. Like all the best plans, it worked. So, they would seemingly disappear completely until July and August 2002 when, at Ed's suggestion, they took what Colin—who had recently taken up baking—described as a "Creative Gentlemen's Leisurely Tour" of Portugal and Spain. The good people of the Iberian Peninsula would surely not have been surprised to discover that, as ever, quiet Radiohead had not meant idle Radiohead. As Rachel Owen continued studying for her PhD on Dante's *Inferno*, Thom had become an expert in feeding and wiping Noah (the newfound domesticity didn't extend to DIY: Thom doesn't do DIY) and, still unable to read music, he crafted skeletons of songs. "I wasn't working," he insisted, "I wasn't really writing." Before Portugal, they had spent nine weeks rehearsing sixteen new songs, without computers and

I MIGHT BE WRONG: LIVE RECORDINGS

RECORDED AT Vaison-la-Romaine, Provence-Alpes-Côte d'Azur, France; South Park, Oxford, England; Blossom Music Center, Cuyahoga Falls, OH; Oslo Spektrum, Oslo, Norway

ENGINEERED & MIXED BY Nigel Godrich, Will Shapland & Jim Warren

PERSONNEL
Thom Yorke
Jonny Greenwood
Colin Greenwood
Ed O'Brien
Philip Selway

COVER ART
Tchock & Stanley

RELEASED November 12, 2001

LABEL Parlophone, CDFHEIT 45104

TRACK LIST
The National Anthem
I Might Be Wrong
Morning Bell
Like Spinning Plates
Idioteque
Everything in Its Right Place
Dollars and Cents
True Love Waits

"It might prove more durable than its parents." Q

almost without Thom's newfound love for both Jamaican dancehall and *Everyone Knows This Is Nowhere*-era Neil Young. This time, there were proper lyrics and they would eventually make the new album's sleeve, albeit with the footnote "These Lyrics contain certain Words that some People may find Offensive."

Other than a neutrals-pleasing set at the Benicàssim Festival, they opened shows with seven or eight new songs, before delving into the back catalog and resurrecting "Lift" once again. Even "Creep" was dusted off in Porto. "There There" would begin with Thom and Ed on tom-toms and the whole enterprise was a return to their pre-*Kid A* template of road-testing before going into the studio. "We are," promised Thom, "going to make a shagging record, if you like to shag very slowly, at 80 bpm."

In September 2002, after very tentative efforts at recording, Radiohead and Nigel Godrich went to Hollywood's Ocean Way to record. The suggestion was the producer's, but the enthusiasm for the trip was the band's. "Last time, we went to Copenhagen thinking, 'Our music needs snow, cold and darkness,'" Jonny told *Q*. "It was a wretched way to think. This time we went for sun and warmth: now there's something we haven't tried before." Dope was smoked, Minis were hired, and clubs were visited, but the studio booking was for a fortnight and that's all it took: fourteen days, midday to midnight. Nigel Godrich stayed on to do some mixing. He was intermittently assisted by Thom, who flew over to play solo sets at both nights of Neil Young's annual Bridge School Benefit Concert. On the first night Thom covered "After the Gold Rush," playing the piano on which Young had recorded the original. "Before you go on, you have to hang out with the other musicians," Thom lamented. "I'm not very good in these situations so I prepared myself by drinking heavily."

Then, everyone returned to Canned Applause for a longer—but still blink-of-an-eye by Radiohead standards—period of additional recording and mixing. *Hail to the Thief* would be their Hollywood album, but it's the Hollywood of the night, of the vampires who suck young blood, of Griffith Park Observatory at sunset, and of the gloaming. In fact, the album was almost called "The Gloaming" and hindsight suggests it was a better option, and certainly one which didn't tie the album to its gestation period. Tellingly, Thom still sometimes refers to it as "The Gloaming."

Hail to the Thief's actual title came from George W. Bush's still-disputed election of 2000, plus Thom's love of *Being There*, the Peter Sellers satire where an idiot becomes President. The artwork—Thom was now Dr Tchock, while Stanley Donwood had accompanied the band to California—was a Hollywood streetmap and the words were taken from street advertising. Thom would always deny it was a protest album, claiming instead that it concerns "the accumulation of power by the very few."

It didn't seem like it at the time, but *I Might Be Wrong: Live Recordings* was another full stop, the end of both Radiohead's electronica period (although, much as he claimed to have stopped listening to techno and started tuning into Radio 4, the UK's flagship news station, Thom's solo albums show he remains unsated) and their stress-inducing make-it-up-in-the-studio phase. The *Hail to the Thief* sessions went smoothly by Radiohead standards, and while Thom's description of them being "like a holiday camp" was pushing it, he wasn't pushing it by much. Rather than analyzing everything each day, they recorded, moved on, and came back later. "On *Kid A* we were in a bad, paranoid place and I really don't like *Amnesiac*," Ed told *Q*. "Now, it's fucking brilliant: there's space, sunshine and energy in the songs. You haven't heard energy from us for a long time. We're cashing in the karma chips."

Maybe it was the familiarity of Canned Applause, or maybe they couldn't quite believe that a recording session could be so painless, but there was more work to be done than they'd anticipated. Mixing took an age and the initial release date of February 2003 was soon forgotten, which made the March leak of what the band said was an unfinished draft even more galling. A more feasible date was June, usually a dead month in terms of new albums, although it hadn't harmed *Amnesiac*. Thom and Rachel Owen were married in May in conditions of such secrecy it's a wonder the Stasi didn't officiate. In fact, maybe they did, for those who were there have kept shtoom to this day. Later that month, the creative gentlemen toured smaller venues, this time opening with fewer new songs (three in Dublin; "There There" and "2 + 2 = 5" everywhere else), but more were unfurled as the sets progressed.

Another promise of a return to guitars, plus Ed's prediction that "it won't alienate people," and Thom's that it would be "a sparkly, shiny pop record, clear and pretty," implied that *Hail to the Thief* would not be a great leap forward. As a result, the sense of anticipation that heralded the radical curveballs that were *OK Computer* and *Kid A* wasn't there. Because there were no war stories to tell of its making; because the wheel remained un-reinvented; because it was a summer, baby; because Jonny was too late saying to *NME* it was about "confusion, avoiding things, looking after yourself and your family" it has been subsumed by the fireworks of the rest of the Radiohead canon. Unfairly so, mostly.

Consciously mimicking Victorian playbills, each song title had an explanatory alternative title, but the first track, recorded on the first day at Ocean Way, "2 + 2 = 5" (aka the Dante-referencing "The Lukewarm"), and the first track on the album itself, began with a joke. Led Zeppelin's Robert Plant sometimes opens solo shows with what sounds very much like the introduction to "Stairway to Heaven." Then he mock-chides his band, who instantly revert into something newer and solo. Radiohead did much the same thing here: The discordant, scratchy opening suggested we were back in *Kid A* territory, before it was shoved aside by a lovely curly introduction not a million miles from Texas's "Say What You

Want" and some bustling verses, before the biggest Radiohead chorus since "Anyone Can Play Guitar."

Hail to the Thief's most difficult track to nail, "Sit Down Stand Up" (aka "Snakes & Ladders"), was a rare older song. Thom claims to have written it while watching coverage of the Rwanda genocide, placing its initial lyrical gestation between *Pablo Honey* and *The Bends*. Either way, by 1998 there was music and, shortly afterwards, a snail's pace demo, but the final version ended with a tsunami of programmed electronica. The speculated return to rock? Hardly.

Jonny's initial judgement on "Sail to the Moon" (aka "Brush the Cobwebs out of the Sky," which refers to a song from "Flying," an episode of *Bagpuss*, the mid-seventies British children's program Thom had read to Noah) was that "It wasn't well-written until the whole band figured out how the structures should be," although the final version was echo-laden but unashamedly minimal. Phil and Colin were more appreciative of a simple ballad written while Rachel Owen was pregnant, which echoed Bob Dylan's "Forever Young" with its hope that "Maybe you'll be President, but know right from wrong." With the best will in the world, it didn't really go anywhere.

Vaguely anti-Tony Blair, originally conceived during a snowstorm in Japan, and more evidence that computers hadn't been wholly discarded, "Backdrifts" (aka the disappointment of the newly married that the "Honeymoon Is Over") was an ideal fit for *Kid A*, but it added new layers of color to *Hail to the Thief*. Indeed, they were still so unsure where to take it that it didn't make the Iberian tour, but once Thom had finished the ever-evolving lyrics and Jonny had fashioned a busy backdrop, the little gem was polished off quickly.

Nigel Godrich's deadline whip-cracking was a benison to "Go to Sleep" (aka "Little Man Being Erased"). According to Thom, the lyrics were "obviously nonsense" but time constraints meant the tinkerman could tinker no more. Very soon Thom was describing those very same lyrics as "the ones I'm most proud of on the record." They may have been processed, but Jonny's Peter Buck-style guitars wouldn't have been out of place on a Black Crowes album.

"Where I End and You Begin" (aka "The Sky Is Falling In," which referenced Henny Penny or Chicken Little, Thom's favorite childhood bedtime story which, naturally, he also read to Noah) had something of *The Bends*'s stomach-tightening euphoria, but Radiohead didn't let it lie there, referencing that most allegorical of novels *Gulliver's Travels* and adding their most uplifting backing vocals since "(Nice Dream)."

The Gucci little piggy of "Paranoid Android" resurfaced on "We Suck Young Blood" (originally "Bring on the New Blood," aka "Your Time is Up"), another *Kid A*-period effort, more specifically Thom's hand-clapping Charles Mingus infatuation. This time, unlike the contemporaneous "Pyramid Song," the woozy, staccato handclaps were retained and they enhance a song already bristling with mischief and invention. With such eyebrow-raising authenticity that Thom insisted the song was a joke ("well, it makes me laugh"), he once again flung himself into Los Angeles's underbelly, and Colin saw it as a potshot at "multi-platinum artists linking up with the latest French disco producer. Radiohead will never be that desperate." Madonna's thoughts on this song remain unrecorded.

Hail to the Thief's centerpiece was "The Gloaming" (aka "Softly Open Our Mouths in the Cold"), another idea that was tossed around during the *Kid A* sessions. Eventually, it evolved into another Noah song concerning, Thom told *NME*, "the feeling I had where we're entering an age of intolerance and fear. I was worrying about what was going to be there when I was gone and Noah was left." One of the few songs which owed more to Oxfordshire than Hollywood, it was still unfinished when they toured Portugal and Spain, but as subtle as it was angry, this was Radiohead at their most ambitious and brave. Still.

HAIL TO THE THIEF

RECORDED AT Ocean Way Recording, Hollywood, California; Canned Applause, Didcot

PRODUCED BY Nigel Godrich & Radiohead

PERSONNEL

Thom Yorke: voice, words, guitar, piano, laptop
Jonny Greenwood: guitar, analogue systems, ondes Martenot, laptop, toy piano, glockenspiel
Colin Greenwood: bass, string synth, sampler
Ed O'Brien: guitar, effects, voice
Philip Selway: drums, percussion

COVER ART

Stanley Donwood: painting, packaging

RELEASED Jun 9, 2003

LABEL Parlophone, 584 5432

HIGHEST CHART POSITION ON RELEASE UK 1, US 3, FRA 1, NZ 3, SWI 3, AUS 2, GER 3, SWE 6

TRACK LIST

2 + 2 = 5. (The Lukewarm.)
Sit Down. Stand Up. (Snakes & Ladders.)
Sail to the Moon. (Brush the Cobwebs out of the Sky.)
Backdrifts. (Honeymoon is Over.)
Go To Sleep. (Little Man Being Erased.)
Where I End and You Begin. (The Sky is Falling in.)
We Suck Young Blood. (Your Time is Up.)
The Gloaming. (Softly Open our Mouths in the Cold.)
There There. (The Boney King of Nowhere.)
I Will. (No Man's Land.)
A Punchup at a Wedding. (No No No No No No No No.)
Myxomatosis. (Judge, Jury & Executioner.)
Scatterbrain. (As Dead as Leaves.)
A Wolf at the Door. (It Girl. Rag Doll.)

"We are going to make a shagging record, if you like to shag very slowly, at 80 bpm." THOM

If any *Hail to the Thief* moment pointed the way to the future, it was the airship-like, percussion-propelled but lush-sounding "There There" (aka "The Boney King of Nowhere," a character who couldn't sit down in "The Owls of Athens," another *Bagpuss* episode), a No. 4 single in the UK. Thom burst into tears when he heard the final mix, as did young Noah when he saw his dad turn into a tree in the video, which was filmed in Fifty Acre Wood, near Bristol.

After a failed attempt to record it in Copenhagen, "I Will" (aka "No Man's Land") was pilfered for *Amnesiac*'s "Like Spinning Plates," but Colin kept rooting for it. Meanwhile, Thom was still haunted by its lyrical starting-point: the US laser-guided bombing of the Amiriyah shelter in Iraq in February 1991 during the first Gulf War, which killed hundreds of women and children. A full band version from Ocean Way was rejected, but back in Oxfordshire, Thom's almost wholly solo version pleased everyone. He was speaking softly but carrying a big stick: "It's the angriest thing I've ever written. The rage is almost inexpressible: it's absolutely primal: you can do anything you like, but if you fuck with my family, I'm not responsible for my actions."

No Radiohead song sounds less like its title than "A Punchup at a Wedding" (aka the comma-free "No No No No No No No No"). It's a meandering little thing, powered along by Thom's Steve Winwood-style piano, musically inspired by the ever-wise Rachel Owen suggesting Thom just let things happen, and lyrically by Thom's more petulant distress at a bad review of the South Park homecoming which, ever over-sensitive, he claimed ruined their day, much as a punch-up might ruin a wedding. The song swings, but the others surely toyed with kiboshing a lyric which included "you had to piss on our parade." Some things you just never outgrow, even when you're the biggest band in the world.

In contrast, the ferocious "Myxomatosis" (aka "Judge, Jury & Executioner") is in-your-face, experimental Radiohead, albeit a

Radiohead familiar with the work of Tubeway Army or, as Thom more readily admitted, Add N to (X). As he noted with relish: "It's the nasty one." Another *Kid A* refugee—some of the lyrics were in that album's CD booklet—it began as a Thom short story, which was expanded into musings on mind control, before incorporating a joke at the expense of British conspiracy theorist David Icke who believes the British royal family are lizards. It was another Los Angeles failure, Oxfordshire success.

Like their humor, Radiohead's warmth is often passed over. With its twinkling melody, "Scatterbrain" (aka "As Dead as Leaves") is as warm as they get, even when the protagonist walks into a storm and gets electrocuted. Thom found it "reassuring"; Jonny was less keen.

Nobody was quite sure whether "A Wolf at the Door" (formerly "Keep the Wolf from the Door," aka "It Girl, Rag Doll") would make the album, not because of its baroque introduction or Thom's unusually rasping vocals, but because its violent lyric was so direct. There was even a (sort of) toasting section, where Thom reminded us that he is, in so many ways, no Buju Banton. Of course, Thom had more than one explanation of what it was about. Either it followed him being beaten up in Oxford, or a late-night train journey with some boorish city boys in first class, or a warning lullaby to Noah. "It was," he concluded, "a basic documentation of the closest I came to a nervous breakdown."

Hail to the Thief was a UK chart-topper and a No. 3 in the US, but for the first time since *Pablo Honey*, there was an absence of perceived genius, be it the actual genius of *The Bends* and *OK Computer* or the sense of geniuses at work on *Kid A* and *Amnesiac*. The band didn't help themselves, carping almost to a man that it was too long and too rushed. Critics tended to agree, and even John Harris struggled with it in a three-star *Q* review: "It's dangerously close to being all experimentalism and precious little substance."

Live, they took the easy way out at first. Thom and Jonny did some acoustic performances before the whole band summered on the festival circuit and took a gentle stroll around Italy. They headlined Glastonbury again and everything went to plan. Without a looming crisis, without the need to push boundaries, and with an album wildly different to its predecessor, but no reinvention, it was as if a balloon was slowly deflating.

By mid-August they were touring the United States for the first time in two years, climaxing with two nights at Madison Square Garden, a venue to which they would not return for thirteen years. Before that, there was a twenty-minute-show of improvised samples at the Brooklyn School of Music, where they soundtracked half of Merce Cunningham Dance Company's *Split Sides* ballet. Icelandic imps Sigur Rós did the other half and a roll of the dice determined who went on first. Sigur Rós released their version the following March as the *Ba Ba Ti Ki Di Do* EP. Radiohead decided their contribution wasn't nearly as good and it remains unreleased beyond a *Split Sides* DVD.

A British tour took them up to Christmas, and with the pressure well and truly off ("It's been pretty stable really," shrugged Colin to Australian magazine *The Age*), they took a break, chiefly because they could. "We'd flown the wrong way around the world, east to west," explained Thom to *The Guardian*, as if he'd never been out of Headington before. "You're not built to do that. It spun our heads out, man. I don't think anybody really slept for weeks. That level of sleep deprivation and doing big shows under a lot of pressure was messed up. It was getting boring, a bit weird and self-perpetuating. It felt like everyone was under obligation to do it rather than because we wanted to." How times had changed.

"On Kid A we were in a bad, paranoid place and I really don't like Amnesiac. Now, it's fucking brilliant: there's space, sunshine and energy in the songs. You haven't heard energy from us for a long time. We're cashing in the karma chips." ED

Throwing shapes at the Empress Ballroom, Blackpool, 12 May, 2006.

9
HOW MUCH WOULD YOU LIKE TO PAY, SIR?

Radiohead's first lost year, 2004, began with Ed and wife Susan Kobrin's first child, Salvador, arriving in January and in March there was the contract-completing *Hail to the Thief* B-sides compilation, *Com Lag (2plus2isfive)*, which stumbled to No. 37 in the British charts. In April there were four shows in Japan, three in Australia, and on May 1, a Coachella Festival headline, after which Thom decided he wanted to leave the band, as did Ed. In the face of such nonsense, they agreed to stop seeing each other for a while. Phil and Jonny took cameos as band members in *Harry Potter and the Goblet of Fire*.

Towards the end of the year, Thom and Jonny guested on Band Aid 20's "Do They Know It's Christmas?" update, as a favor to producer Nigel Godrich. Significantly, they did not sing and they would wriggle out of playing Live 8 the following year: "I didn't agree with the idea," admitted Thom. "It was a form of distraction." Thom also turned down a meeting with Tony Blair: "They wanted pre-meetings to know I was on-side. It was the illest I ever got. I got so freaked out about it."

The Most Gigantic Lying Mouth of All Time was a DVD compilation of highlights from their Internet station *Radiohead Television*, which began in 2003. Thom's second child, Agnes Mair, was born and he spent much of it writing "things that didn't fit in the Radiohead zone." He wasn't joking here. The man who was constantly on the move, the man who never looked back, would never leave electronica or the Warp sound and his solo albums would provide an outlet for an area and an era his bandmates had long discarded.

On the surface, 2005 was Radiohead's second lost year, but this time appearances were deceptive. Thom finished his Nigel Godrich-produced solo album and kept it on the back burner for a wee while, and there were no interviews or proper band concerts. They were not indolent though. In May 2004, Jonny had become composer-in-residence with the BBC Concert Orchestra, and eleven months later, his first piece with them "Popcorn Superhet Receiver," a nineteen-minute amalgam of Krzysztof Penderecki's "Threnody for the Victims of Hiroshima" and radio squiggles, was premiered in London. Jonny collaborated with the London Sinfonietta at the Ether Festival at London's Royal Festival Hall, performing their first joint effort "Smear" and world-premiering "Piano for Children," alongside pieces by modernist composers. He was joined by Thom on the new "Arpeggi" and, better still, the "There There" B-side "Where Bluebirds Fly," accompanied by an ondes Martenot sextet as Thom hummed the wordless melody.

A new Radiohead song? Oh yes. They had been rehearsing new material since March and recording at Canned Applause in April without Nigel Godrich. On September 8, Thom recorded the beautiful "I Want None of This" for *Help! A Day in the Life*, the latest War Child compilation and credited it to the band. When Thom played a solo piano session in November for *From the Basement*, a program Nigel Godrich had created for Sky Arts, there was another new song, "Videotape." The whole band would return to *From the Basement*.

At the end of 2005, they hired prolific producer Mark "Spike" Stent who'd worked for The Spice Girls, Oasis, Madonna, and U2 among dozens of A-listers. It seemed like an odd, Zeitgeist-chasing move. Sessions were booked for February.

"Apart from *Hail to the Thief*, all these records we made with Nigel were in the comfort zone," Ed told Radio 1 just before Christmas, a statement of almost surreal bizarreness. "You've got to get out of that. We've been working together for ten years, we need our relationship. We all love one another too much."

Thom had a Dizzee Rascal phase; Colin discovered go-ahead indie label XL's The White Stripes; and by April, Radiohead were promising a "minimal" album which would include "Nude," which they'd been playing since 1998. Thom was cagey about its release date. The inevitable split with Mark "Spike" Stent surprised only the band. "Everyone had lost . . . not interest, but momentum," Thom told *Rolling Stone*. "We'd all stopped to have kids. When we got back into the studio, it was just dead." With the sessions in danger of emulating *Kid A*'s difficult birth, they did what they usually did in such situations and found catharsis on the road, integrating new tracks such as "15 Step" and "House of Cards" chiefly in Britain, although the second of two shows in Amsterdam was cancelled when Phil's mother, Thea, died. Two days later, he was back onstage. During another exhaustive American trek, Thom instigated the scrapping of everything they'd recorded and, not wholly uncontentiously, the return of Nigel Godrich.

Not a man to vary some parts of a winning formula, in September and October Nigel Godrich whisked the band to Tottenham House, a stately home in Wiltshire, south of Oxford, where the multimillionaires would sleep in caravans. They would move on to another stately home, Halswell House before completing at The Hospital, Nigel Godrich's London studio and Canned Applause. "Things came together when Nigel started working with us again," admitted Colin. "He was someone we knew we had to be accountable to. Before then it was pie in the sky." Having reassessed what they had over Christmas 2006, their traditional late surge of creativity and industry meant they were finished by late spring 2007. Jonny celebrated that and his recently kindled love of reggae by compiling the uproarious *Jonny Greenwood is the Controller*, to celebrate the fortieth anniversary of the Trojan label. Stanley Donwood did the cover and tracks included Delroy Wilson's jawdropping "This Life Makes Me Wonder" and Derrick Harriott's righteous "Let Me Down Easy." Meanwhile, Thom sang "The White Flash" for German electro duo Modeselektor. Four years later, they would reunite on "Shipwreck" and "This."

That the *Com Lag (2plus2isfive)* filler was their last album of their EMI deal weighed heavy. On A Friday had signed in 1991 and Keith Wozencroft was still there, as Capitol/Virgin UK President. Other pivotal relationships had been formed with Parlophone MD Tony Wadsworth and Parlophone PR Murray Chalmers. The days of demands for hit singles and for albums which met EMI-imposed deadlines were gone, if not wholly forgotten by the band. Globe-straddling success meant the scales were as tipped as they had been with the press a long time ago. Where once the band worked for the label, now the label worked for the band. And yet the label owned the band's catalog.

Significantly, when Thom's electronica solo album, *The Eraser*, finally arrived in July 2006, between the American and European legs of Radiohead's tour, it arrived on XL Recordings. "I want no crap about me being a traitor or splitting up blah blah," Thom told his fans' information service "and I don't want to hear the word 'solo.'" XL, the company built on Adele's sales, had the clout to take this unashamedly uncommercial diversion dedicated to Agnes Mair to No. 3 in the British charts and a remarkable No. 2 in America.

Allied to this, something else, something more mercurial, was ticking away in the background. For the first time, the music industry was changing faster than music itself. All major labels were paralyzed by their inability to monetize streaming, downloading, and anything to do with the Internet. The value of music was plummeting, not least because—as the *Hail to the Thief* leak demonstrated—it was no longer something consumers assumed they should pay for. As he was with most things, Thom was intrigued, scared, and wearied:

One of the weirdest things was us working incredibly hard on Hail to the Thief—*as usual, too hard—and then seeing the music business going into meltdown and diminishing the value of what we do. It's frightening. There's nothing I can do about it. It sounds really precious, but it's doing my head in. It's stopping me knowing where to go next. Music has always been a commodity, but now it's a commodity that's almost free. I always felt it was more valuable than that and it feels cheap and disposable. It's like, "I'll download 50 tracks, listen to them once and then throw them away." I find that depressing. I am now one of many, many content providers: but I've never seen it like that. Music is a sacred thing.*

The storm was about to break. While Radiohead had cheerily referred to themselves as an unsigned band throughout 2006, in 2007 EMI still believed Radiohead would renew their deal. As late as August, Tony Wadsworth could be found in Oxfordshire, loving the new material in anticipation of that renewal. However, that month EMI was acquired by private equity company Terra Firma for £4.2 billion. Radiohead had already secretly made the decision not to go with EMI, but the prospect of a company with no music industry experience being their overlords erased all doubts.

As EMI tentatively planned for a 2008 release, on September 30, 2007, Jonny blogged the bomb: "The new album is finished and it's coming out in 10 days. We've called it *In Rainbows*. Love from us all."

They had informed Tony Wadsworth the previous day. The circle around the band had remained so tight, even after all this time, that EMI simply didn't know what was afoot. A music man to his core, Tony Wadsworth was broken by both the lack of trust the band had shown in Parlophone and by extension him, not to mention his own, naive willingness to trust them. By January, the former guitarist in the Young Bucks had ended his twenty-five-year association with EMI as Terra Firma cut two thousand jobs.

As Thom wrestled with his fears of music becoming worthless, there was more. In fact, Radiohead hadn't signed to another label as EMI had feared, with the paranoia of a spurned husband/wife fearing their former partner finding someone else. Sick of the leaking culture (it even affected *The Eraser*), the media jockeying for exclusivity, and an album being defined by its pre-release reviews, Radiohead were desperate to do something different. They did: they made *In Rainbows* available on their website as a download. At Chris Hufford's insistence, it would cost whatever the downloader wished to pay. They had destroyed the music industry. Heavens.

Thom insisted to none other than David Byrne in *Wired* that "It's not supposed to be a model, it was simply a response to a situation. We're out of contract. We have our own studio. We have a new server." However, the ripples for less popular artists spread far and wide. Never again would the release of an album—the industry's mainstay since *Rubber Soul*, the fans' lifeblood, the acts' calling card—mean quite so much. It's an exaggeration to suggest that popular music has never recovered, but not by much.

There would be an *In Rainbows* CD, but EMI would not release it. Terra Firma boss Guy Hands was a businessman, rather than a music man. He was open to Radiohead leasing their new product to EMI—after all Kraftwerk had been doing it with EMI for decades via their Kling Klang Produkt imprint. However, Guy Hands was not open to the band regaining their catalog. Without their history, Radiohead would not budge. The divorce was absolute.

Ed argued that "Terra Firma doesn't understand the music industry," which was true, although they were adhering to standard practice here. Terra Firma countered that Radiohead were greedy. "At our valuation, they wanted millions and millions," claimed Guy Hands. "We just weren't going to do it: we couldn't make money on what they wanted."

Naturally, Thom was unrepentant and his high horse was saddled: "We wanted control over our work and how it was used in the future. That seemed reasonable to us, as we care about it a great deal."

In December, Jonny released his soundtrack to Paul Thomas Anderson's *There Will Be Blood*. With its Sharona Katan sleeve, it might have won an Oscar had it not unfathomably included snatches of the previously released "Popcorn Superhet Receiver" and some of *Bodysong*, therefore rendering it ineligible. That month, a fortnight before *In Rainbows*'s UK release on CD by XL, EMI released a box set of the first six studio albums and *I Might Be Wrong: Live Recordings*. "It fucking ruined my Christmas," muttered Thom.

"We don't have a huge amount of reasons to be nice to them. We need the money for the bank. If it spoiled his Christmas, I'm sorry!" countered Guy Hands, with the air of a man who wasn't really sorry at all.

In fact, Radiohead have always been good with money. Their accounts are a byzantine jungle of active and dissolved companies, and the age-old tale of the naive musician being ripped off by unscrupulous men in suits has never applied.

Since 1993, when Radiohead Ltd made a $25 loss on a $264,746 turnover, their touring company's turnover increased to $1,075,891 in 1995, $3 million in 1997, and $11.7 million in 2003. The company would be liquidated in 2013, so that solvent it had $2.13 million in assets. There are separate companies for merchandising, and since they established Xurbia Xendless to deal with *In Rainbows*'s income, a new company has been created for almost every new project.

Hail to the Thief had probably been the moment when Radiohead realized that while their fan base was super-loyal, for now there were no vast untapped reservoirs of appreciation. They no longer needed a record company to proselytize on their behalf, something which partially explains *In Rainbows*'s release. Xurbia Xendless was soon overloaded with downloads. In the first month, over a million people downloaded *In Rainbows*, paying an average of $6. With no middleman to take a cut, it netted the band $3 million. Most people took it for nothing, but fifteen paid £99.99.

Somewhere along this road, the music of *In Rainbows* had been sacrificed. For all that its arrival was sudden and different, it's rehearse, then record, then road-test, then twiddle genesis was vintage Radiohead. As noted, for reasons still not wholly clear, all the band thought *Hail to the Thief* was too long, so of sixteen available songs (eighteen if we include the hummed "MK1," which was built from parts of "Videotape" and the lovely, brief instrumental "MK2"), ten were selected for *In Rainbows*. The remaining, lesser, tracks were gathered on a twenty-seven-minute bonus disc box edition, which sold 100,000 copies and grossed £8 million.

Distractions aside, it's a beautiful, innovative collection, although the truly groundbreaking aspect came from those release-based distractions. There's a joke in the opening "15 Step": "You used to be alright, what happened? Et cetera, et cetera," and there's a musical one, too, similar to "2 + 2 = 5," as it begins in scratchy electro fashion before soaring into clipped, almost tidal joy. The children's choir chanting "Hey!" were from the Matrix Music School in Sutton Courtenay recorded when Colin and Nigel Godrich dropped in.

IN RAINBOWS

RECORDED AT Tottenham House, Marlborough; Halswell House, Taunton; Hospital Studios, London; Radiohead Oxfordshire studio

PRODUCED BY Nigel Godrich & Radiohead

PERSONNEL
Colin Greenwood
Ed O'Brien
Jonny Greenwood
Phil Selway
Thom Yorke

ADDITIONAL PERSONNEL
The Millennia Ensemble: strings
Matrix Music School children's choir: uncredited choir on "15 Step"

COVER ART
Stanley Donwood & Dr Tchock

RELEASED Oct 10, 2007 (_Xurbia_Xendless Limited) & Dec 31, 2007 (XL Recordings)

LABEL _Xurbia_Xendless Limited, DL_X_X001 & XL Recordings, XLLP 324

HIGHEST CHART POSITION ON RELEASE UK 1, US 1, FRA 1, NZ 2, CAN 1, SWI 2, AUS 2, ITA 7, GER 8, SPA 19, NL 7, JAP 11

TRACK LIST
15 Step
Bodysnatchers
Nude
Weird Fishes/Arpeggi
All I Need
Faust Arp
Reckoner
House of Cards
Jigsaw Falling into Place
Videotape

The special edition of In Rainbows included a second disc, In Rainbows Disk 2, which contains eight additional tracks.

MK 1
Down Is the New Up
Go Slowly
MK 2
Last Flowers
Up on the Ladder
Bangers + Mash
4 Minute Warning

"If Thom claimed Hail To The Thief was a 'shagging' album, he described In Rainbows as a 'seduction'."

With its harsh guitars, rhythmic distortion, lyrics loosely inspired by *The Stepford Wives*, and furious pace, Thom reckoned "Bodysnatchers" was part Krautrockers Neu! and part Australian mavericks Wolfmother. He was right. On an album of galleons, this was a speedboat.

Regarded as something of a "Lift"-style lost gem since it was first mooted for *OK Computer*, "Nude" missed the *Kid A/Amnesiac* and *Hail to the Thief* cuts when it was titled "Big Ideas (Don't Get Any)," but when Colin gave it a new, muscular bassline and Thom stopped singing it like a hostage, it was finally deemed worthy. "Luminous" is the word.

Originally titled just "Arpeggi" (as in "arpeggio") when it was played at Ether by Thom and Jonny, "Weird Fishes/Arpeggi" was the most complex moment of *In Rainbows*, with Jonny and Ed battling to impose themselves over Thom's understated vocals and Phil's chugging rhythm. So tense are the verses that it's one of the few Radiohead songs which would have been enhanced by a cathartic chorus.

In contrast, "All I Need" didn't need a chorus at all. Thom was singing of obsession, but this was Jonny's moment. He recruited the Millennia Ensemble string section (they'd be credited, unlike the Matrix kids), fresh from Take That's "Rule the World," to add gravitas to an already somber track.

Short and sharp, but an unusually diverting mid-album change of pace, "Faust Arp" (as in the daddy of dada, sculptor Jean Arp) has more Jonny-arranged strings, Thom's knowing lyrics, and some tidal acoustic strumming. It's a piece of muscle-flexing and as Thom equivocated, "I vaguely know the story of Faust . . ."

They hadn't clattered as hard as they did on "Reckoner" since "Airbag." It's very much not to be confused with the "Reckoner" they'd played during the *Amnesiac* tour. The band repeatedly returned to the original "Reckoner," only to discard it again and again. However, Thom and Jonny took the song's ending and built this new "Reckoner" around it. Confusingly, the original would be rehashed as Thom's stand-alone single of 2009, "Feeling Pulled Apart by Horses." Hypnotic, restless, and slowly revealing its capacity for invention and pathos, it's a canon high point. Gnarls Barkley would do a surprisingly faithful cover version.

The Grammy-nominated (for Best Rock Song, Best Music Video, and, deep breath, Best Rock Performance by a Duo or Group with Vocal) "House of Cards" was Radiohead at their wooziest, and it merged a fairly straightforward ballad with unusually quiet electronica. Claiming the allusions to wife-swapping were not taken from personal experience, Thom reckoned this most sensual of Radiohead tracks was "satisfying, really mellow and summery" and that it sounded a little like Fleetwood Mac's "Albatross." Again, he wasn't wrong.

Thom was concerned about "Jigsaw Falling into Place," when it was called "Open Pick." Recorded at Tottenham House, it was one of his Mr Disgusted Visits A Bar lyrics and, rather more rarely since The Bends, it was a three-pronged guitar attack. What is different, though, is that there's sympathy for the barflies. What if a night heading towards oblivion is when the jigsaw falls into place, even if it's for a fleeting moment?

"It's really cool," gushed Thom to Rolling Stone of the closer, "Videotape." Both Thom and Nigel Godrich had wanted their favorite track to open In Rainbows. They were overruled. "It's got lots of cyclical melodies," explained Thom. "It's one of the first things we had. We were smashing our heads against the wall, trying to figure out what to do with it. Sometimes that drives me crazy." It's more closing lullaby than grand encapsulation and it pointed the way ahead.

If Thom claimed Hail to the Thief was a "shagging" album, he described In Rainbows as a "seduction" and the album's title as born of obsession. And there was an absence of despair that he had never really allowed himself before. It doesn't have the band's best songs, but as a whole it's their most beautiful album. Perhaps it was what they had been meaning to say all along.

Phil goes on solo tour, Circolo Degli Artisti, Rome, Italy, 31 March, 2010.

10
LET'S TAKE OUR TIME

They all had at least two children now, and in a world where Thom preferred to spend his Sundays taking his kids to the Oxford University Museum of Natural History, the old urgency evaporated a little more.

As the gig-less year of 2007 drew to a close, they rehearsed, and one blissful day their version of Frankie Valli and the Four Seasons' "The Night" will surely surface. Remarkably, once the pay-what-you-want experiment was over, the CD version of *In Rainbows*—XL in the UK; TBD in the US—topped the British and American charts, but such was the messy nature of its arrival that Radiohead elected not to tour it properly until May 2008.

Before that, April began with a couple of BBC shows which the national radio networks would cannibalize. A day later, there was a return to Nigel Godrich's *From the Basement* show at The Hospital. Here, in a performance that transcended its sterile setting, they aired all of *In Rainbows* bar "Faust Arp" and "Jigsaw Falling Into Place," while they took two very different tilts at "House of Cards," one solely for *Late Night With Conan O'Brien*; an opportunity for Thom to mention how much CO_2 they'd saved by not flying to New York. This was the moment where *In Rainbows* began to make sense live.

There were legitimate distractions. Jonny had the US premiere of "Popcorn Superhet Receiver" to oversee and Colin played bass on the score to Alex Karpovsky's comedy *Woodpecker*. No matter, they took a quick spin around American amphitheaters; Thom released *The Eraser*

Rmxs, a remix of *The Eraser*. They played the European/US festival circuit in the summer and Japan in October.

They didn't play "Creep" that year, but Prince did, a mighty, eight-and-a-half-minutes version at Coachella. When Ed went to watch it on YouTube, Prince had blocked it. "Hang on, it's our song," said Thom. "Tell him to unblock it." Prince obeyed. It's still there today.

EMI had been busy too. June saw *Radiohead: The Best Of*, available as a single CD, a double CD, or a DVD. "If we'd been behind it, it would have been good," sniffed Thom, who, for the first and last time, helped out kid brother Andy, singer of the far from feted Unbelievable Truth, on a cover of Miracle Legion's "All for the Best," a track on *Ciao My Shining Star*, a tribute to Miracle Legion singer Mark Mulcahy. In March 2009, EMI reissued *Pablo Honey*, *The Bends*, and *OK Computer*, un-remastered, but with an extra disc of assorted B-sides, remixes, BBC versions, and live tracks. For the more committed, there was an additional DVD. *Kid A*, *Amnesiac* and *Hail to the Thief* followed in August. The band remained unimpressed. Fans were much more ambivalent.

Perhaps Radiohead's urgency hadn't evaporated after all. Perhaps they just needed a rest and a broadening of horizons. As early as May 2009, still worker bees at heart, they returned to the studio with Nigel Godrich between South American and European festival dates. By August, they were back on the road and, as is the Radiohead way, there was the occasional airing of a new song, "These Are My Twisted Words," which was eventually given away as a free download a fortnight after "Harry Patch (In Memory Of)," a tribute to the last surviving World War I British soldier, for which they charged £1 per download and donated the profits to veterans' organization the Royal British Legion.

Times were changing. Phil had been pondering a solo album since 2006 and now the moment had come. Thom had belatedly decided that *The Eraser* needed to meet its public, so he formed a new band that would eventually be called Atoms for Peace, after a track on *The Eraser* which quoted a Dwight Eisenhower speech to the United Nations. Nigel Godrich joined, as did Red Hot Chili Peppers bassist Flea, session drummer extraordinaire Joey Waronker, and David Byrne's Brazilian percussionist Mauro Refosco. The then-unnamed band played three October nights in Los Angeles. The shows comprised *The Eraser* in its entirety, correct running order and all, plus a Thom solo acoustic encore, then both sides of the "Feeling Pulled Apart by Horses"/"The Hollow Earth" single, the Radiohead B-side "Paperbag Writer," and the wholly new "Judge, Jury and Executioner," which Thom had apparently forgotten had been the alternative title to "Myxomatosis." In December he was in Copenhagen, a frustrated figure at the UN Climate Change Conference ("I was obsessed, with good reason. I couldn't look at my little boy and not try to do something"). Amidst all this, a new Radiohead album was on its way. "We've got our chops up," grinned Ed.

A patchy year followed in 2010. Thom co-wrote and guested on Los Angeles electro maverick Flying Lotus's fabulous ". . . And the World Laughs With You" from the Warp album *Cosmogramma*. If the pair didn't physically meet (Thom emailed his vocals in), the skittering but winsome result was a meeting of minds and they reconvened on 2012's "Electric Candyman": "I thought he was done with me," Flying Lotus admitted to *Spin*. "Thom's just a head. He tries to stay up on what's happening. I like it when he gets into that spooky pocket. People say it doesn't sound like Thom, but it's my album."

There was a band benefit for earthquake-ravaged Haiti where Thom played "Lotus Flower" solo. Thom and Jonny were a secret, acoustic addition to Glastonbury and Jonny's twenty-three-minute musical tour diary "Doghouse" premiered, but in truth this was Thom and Phil's year. Thom toured with Atoms for Peace, but Phil surprised everyone with *Familial*, where he called himself Philip, sang, played guitar, recruited Lisa Germano plus Wilco's drummer Glenn Kotche, and wrote ten beautiful, elegiac songs. There was no Nigel Godrich, no Stanley Donwood, and no guest spots from his bandmates, just the sense that someone had been hiding a considerable talent for a considerable amount of time.

Entwined with all this peripheral activity, that new band album was being recorded. Unsettled, but surely unsurprised by *In Rainbows*'s unnecessarily torturous sessions, this time around, they and Nigel Godrich returned to Los Angeles and based themselves at Drew Barrymore's house. As ever, they knew what they didn't want: chords and electronica. As ever, they were less sure what they did want.

Phil had become a patron of Oxford's Pegasus Theatre, who were collaborating on a project with Samaritans. Colin became global ambassador for the Children's Radio Foundation charity, with whom he would visit South Africa in 2012. Ed had discovered Australian psychedelic ace Tame Impala, but with Thom engrossed by Hans Fallada's recently exhumed novel *Alone in Berlin* and returning to DJing for the first time since Exeter, chiefly at Los Angeles's electronica temple Low End Theory, the band settled on sampling themselves and Jonny programmed all the sound-looping software.

"I said, 'Okay, let's do an experiment for two weeks where everyone has a turntable instead of playing guitar or drums or whatever,'" explained Nigel Godrich to *Rolling Stone*. "That two-week experiment ended up being fucking six months. That's that record, the whole story of all of it." They called it *The King of Limbs*, since, argued Ed incomprehensibly, it's a rhythm record and rhythm is the king of limbs. More likely, it could refer to a thousand-year-old oak tree in Savernake Forest, Wiltshire, very near Tottenham House. Oh, and it's there in chapter twenty-three of The Qur'an: "Heart is the king of limbs and so if one intends to pray whole-heartedly, the limbs will follow the heart."

THE KING OF LIMBS

RECORDED AT Drew Barrymore's home, Los Angeles, California

PRODUCED BY Nigel Godrich & Radiohead

PERSONNEL
Colin Greenwood
Ed O'Brien
Jonny Greenwood
Phil Selway
Thom Yorke

ADDITIONAL PERSONNEL
Noel Langley: flugelhorn on "Bloom" and "Codex"
Yazz Ahmed: flugelhorn on "Bloom" and "Codex"
The London Telefilmonic Orchestra: strings on "Codex"

COVER ART
Donald Twain (Stanley Donwood) & Zachariah Wildwood (Thom Yorke)

RELEASED Feb 18, 2011 (self-release) & Mar 28, 2011 (XL Recordings)

LABEL XL Recordings, TICK001CD

HIGHEST CHART POSITION ON RELEASE UK 7, US 3, FRA 8, NZ 5, CAN 5, SWI 8, AUS 2, ITA 8, GER 13, SPA 10, JAP 3

TRACK LIST
Bloom
Morning Mr Magpie
Little by Little
Feral
Lotus Flower
Codex
Give up the Ghost
Separator
Bloom

TKOL RMX 1234567, a remix album of songs from the album was released Sept 16, 2011 in Japan and Oct 10, 2011 internationally by XL Recordings

Little By Little (Caribou Rmx)
Lotus Flower (Jacques Greene Rmx)
Morning Mr Magpie (Nathan Fake Rmx)
Bloom (Harmonic 313 Rmx)
Bloom (Mark Pritchard Rmx)
Feral (Lone Rmx)
Morning Mr Magpie (Pearson Sound Scavenger Rmx)
Separator (Four Tet Rmx)
Give Up The Ghost (Thriller Houseghost Rmx)
Codex (Illum Sphere Rmx)
Little By Little (Shed Rmx)
Give Up The Ghost (Brokenchord Rmx)
TKOL (Altrice Rmx)
Bloom (Blawan Rmx)
Good Evening Mrs Magpie (Modeselektor Rmx)
Bloom (Objekt Rmx)
Bloom (Jamie xx Rework)
Separator (Anstam Rmx)
Lotus Flower (SBTRKT Rmx)

As Thom suggested, "Almost every tune is like a collage," and the credit would read: "The music and sounds from *The King of Limbs* were conjured up by Radiohead and produced by Nigel Godrich." The shortest Radiohead album—lasting just thirty-seven minutes—would be released in February as a download (for £6: at least one *In Rainbows* lesson had been learned); an ordinary CD via XL and TBD again; and, three months later, as a luxury special edition. Between the two versions, there was the appearance of Jonny's third soundtrack, this time to the Japanese adaption of Haruki Murakami's novel *Norwegian Wood*. At Jonny's insistence, it included three old Can tracks.

There were delicious flugelhorns on the slinky "Bloom," courtesy of Noel Langley from the London Sinfonietta and British-Bahraini Yazz Ahmed, who noted: "Radiohead opened up eyes and ears to using technology in live performance, and using the studio as a compositional tool, manipulating pre-recorded sounds." Phil's percussion couldn't be busier and Thom was inspired by the BBC's natural history series *The Blue Planet*. "That is the most complex, antagonistic, tangled rhythm," commented drummer Clive Deamer, soon to join Radiohead's touring lineup. "It's certainly not pop, certainly not rock. It's got the same intensity as any Sun Ra, or drummer Elvin Jones's bursts with John Coltrane."

"Morning, Mr Magpie," formerly "Mornin' Mi Lord," had been mulled over for almost a decade. There was a clear problem: while Thom's acoustic skeleton was enticing, it was clearly incomplete. The band struggled to add flesh until they settled on an insistent riff and Phil's hi-hat. Lyrically, there's bleakness to spare as Thom details being relieved of magic, memories, melody and other things beginning with "m." Or perhaps it's just an alliterative coincidence.

Radiohead had dispensed with overt hooks for some time, but never covert hooks. *The King of Limbs* was hardly a return to "High & Dry," but "Little by Little" was almost a pop song; in fact, to be more precise, it was almost Tyrannosaurus Rex's "Dwarfish Trumpet Blues." There was a proper chorus, an undulating guitar riff that nodded to a Paul Simon shuffle such as "Late in the Evening," and an intriguing lyric. That it's a place for the uninitiated to start investigating the whole album, doesn't make it less of a song. Quite the opposite and it's the high point of *The King of Limbs* by some distance.

If "Little by Little" flirted with the mainstream, "Feral" was raw Radiohead. Is it an instrumental? Possibly, if unintelligible muttering doesn't count as vocals, but its real fascination is Jonny and Ed battling against each other and against an insistent groove. It's the traditional Radiohead mid-album breather.

Thom had performed "Lotus Flower" during the acoustic encore of his solo shows and, solo again, during the band's Haiti benefit. With the band, it assumed a whole new grandeur, but its nickels and dimes budget video—directed by Garth Jennings, who'd helmed "Nude"—only featured Thom, bowler-hatted, unshaven, sort of miming along to the syncopated beats, sparse verses, and loaded choruses as he dad-danced. An Internet sensation, it was nominated for a Grammy in 2012, as was the song itself (Best Rock Song, Best Rock Performance). The video's Japanese premiere was scheduled to take place in Hachiko Square, Tokyo's Times Square/Piccadilly Circus, but faced with the prospect of overexcited fans imitating Thom's jerky moves, the police intervened to cancel. Thom claims to have turned down an invitation to appear on the BBC's celebrity-based dance competition, *Strictly Come Dancing*.

"Codex" is the album's big piano ballad. Thom is at his most subdued; the backdrop is Radiohead at their most supple and subtle and it could have graced any album after *The Bends*. It's always brave to aspire to beauty ("the water's clear and innocent"), but if you get it right, the world is yours.

Heralded by the birdsong Ed had long adored, "Give Up the Ghost" was another song Thom had played solo. It sounds solo on *The*

King of Limbs, where minimal instrumental backing snuggles up against extensive vocal layering not a million miles away from 10cc's "I'm Not in Love." For a band who devote so much attention to running order, placing this after the not entirely dissimilar "Codex" feels like a ball has been dropped.

Formerly "Mouse Dog Bird," "Separator" is unusually optimistic for a Radiohead album closer and there's a lightness of touch not always found on a challenging album. Sunny uplands are just over the horizon.

Heavily influenced by *The Eraser*, *The King of Limbs* is an unusual combination of the focused and the meandering and it struggled to incite great passion. No. 7 in the US and No. 3 in the UK, it was neither full-stop nor pointer to the way ahead, but it is the album Thom the Exeter student DJ would have made. "It's about breaking out of things," offered Thom, but there's also a life-cycle aspect, with "Bloom" opening and "Give Up the Ghost" the denouement. That its recording was reasonably straightforward and that they did no interviews ("We didn't feel like it," said Ed. "We didn't want to explain it," said Thom.) displayed a lack of confidence rather than another mystique-building exercise. The absence of proper shows around its sudden release meant it passed some people by. These factors combined to ensure it was the first Radiohead album not to strike US gold. "I can see why it alienated people," admitted Thom, a year after its release.

There was no immediate tour but just as *In Rainbows* had shown its true colors at Nigel Godrich's *From the Basement* show, so did *The King of Limbs* when it was aired in its entirety at The Hospital in May. This performance was rustier, less transcendent, but "Supercollider" did get its first airing by the band, having previously been a Thom solo turn. The following month there was a fairly secret, rain-sodden, Glastonbury Park Stage performance where second drummer Clive Deamer made his live debut.

As Phil was the first to observe, *The King of Limbs* would lend itself to remixing and so, in September, shortly before the release of the Jonny-scored *We Need to Talk About Kevin* (the soundtrack was never released: "not long enough," shrugged Jonny), the 2CD, 100-minute remix album *TKOL RMX 1234567* made No. 50 in the US charts. Four Tet worked wonders with "Separator" and Mark Pritchard brought all sorts of new nuance to "Bloom."

Back at the Bonnaroo Music Festival, Manchester, Tennessee, USA, 8 June, 2012.

11
A SORROW SHAPED HOLE

S till shy, Jonny asked someone else to secure Krzysztof Penderecki's autograph when they recorded an album together in Poland. Thom reconvened Atoms for Peace and Radiohead further blended in Clive Deamer on a couple of September 2011 dates at New York's 3,500-capacity Roseland Ballroom. There was even a new song, the Tony Blair-obsessed "The Daily Mail," plus "Supercollider," which hadn't made *The King of Limbs*. The crowd were strangely restless, but Thom was ecstatic after the first night: "It was a fucking trip, the best adrenaline buzz I've had in absolutely years," he told *Rolling Stone*. "It didn't feel like we were treading the old ground, walking over our graves. We were still wandering around in the darkness, stumbling. That was nice." According to the management, the dearth of band shows was a result of Clive Deamer's prior commitment to Portishead. By December, Radiohead were back in the studio.

In contrast, 2012 was a year on the road. February saw their first proper US tour since 2008. The *Drill* EP's twentieth anniversary passed un-commemorated, but there were new songs including "Identikit" and "Ful Stop." *The King of Limbs* tracks blossomed in a live setting and Thom and Ed put their renewed buoyancy down to Clive Deamer's easy-going, hard-drumming presence. Ed suggested that if Radiohead were The Beatles, Clive Deamer was their Billy Preston: "Clive has got people out of old habits. We don't feel like a new band, we feel like a band who knows itself."

The shows were fantastic, but every last drop of optimism evaporated at Downsview Park, Toronto on June 16 when the stage collapsed before the show. It's a rock myth that touring parties are one giant happy family. At Radiohead's level, the traveling carnival employs dozens, but while the band travel as if gently ferried from city to city on a feather-strewn bier piloted by angels, the road crew tends to travel overnight, one twenty-hour day following another, before they slumber at a mid-ranked hotel.

There is though, one intimate relationship: between the musician and his tech. Even the most paranoid musician trusts them intimately. The tech knows the instrument better than the player and, more importantly, they know how the instrument will sound in any given covered or open-air venue or studio. Rotherham-born Scott Johnson was Phil's drum tech, the figure crouched almost out of sight onstage, ready for each and every emergency, after having ensured Phil sounded like a god every evening. When the Toronto stage collapsed, Scott Johnson's head injuries were fatal.

The Canadian authorities instigated legal proceedings against the scaffolding company, the promotors and the engineer, but the case would be thrown out in 2017 after taking too long to come to court. *A Moon Shaped Pool* would be dedicated to Scott Johnson and when Radiohead returned to the city in 2018, Thom was still incandescent: "The people who should be held accountable are not being held accountable in your city. The silence is fucking deafening." Two years later, an inquest at which Phil gave evidence deemed Scott Johnson's death accidental and made twenty-six non-binding recommendations. The band, said Phil afterwards, were distraught, citing "a complete failure of the justice system. The system has failed Scott, his family and other industry workers."

Subsequent European dates were rescheduled, and when they returned to the tour, at Nimes in July, Thom dedicated "Reckoner" to Scott Johnson, whose image was displayed on screen.

The Master, Jonny's tension-laden second soundtrack for Paul Thomas Anderson, was released in September and he trekked to India to study the local music. Even Colin was busy, guesting on Tamino's "Indigo Night": "Colin came to one of my hometown shows in Antwerp," said the Belgian-Egyptian. "We spoke the same musical language and he felt like the perfect match because of his melodic playing, whilst keeping an incredible groove." Colin even dabbled in journalism, reviewing *Erebus: The Story of a Ship* by Monty Python's Michael Palin in right-wing British magazine *The Spectator*: "terrific in its detail, poignant and, with the suggestion of cannibalism, macabre."

Having absorbed the vast catalogs of Fela Kuti and Duke Ellington at Flea's house, Thom finished off the Atoms for Peace album. All the same, for all the industry, a year of rebirth had been wholly overshadowed by one awful, unnecessary death.

Radiohead took 2013 off. Not all of them, of course. In 2007, Ed had said he'd move with his family to Brazil in five years' time. Now he did: "I'd had so many adventures with the band, I wanted to have one with my family," he told the BBC. The O'Briens lived in a hut in the countryside and, gorging on samba, Ed began to write solo material.

Amok, the Atoms For Peace album, arrived in February with a Stanley Donwood sleeve. Culled from extensive studio sessions, and based on feel rather than songs, it would be Thom's attempt to play electronic music with "proper" instruments and it made No. 2 in the US. For all the good intentions, and for all that Flea played a rhythmic blinder, it still sounded like a solo Thom album. He wasn't happy: it wasn't dancey enough, he reckoned; the tracks were too short, he mused; but he still volunteered to tour the world with it. "I don't ever stop working," he admitted to *Dazed & Confused* with more rue than hubris. Spending an hour a day on yoga made things better. For now.

Radiohead took 2014 off, too. Not all of them, of course. In September, Thom released *Tomorrow's Modern Boxes*, another Nigel Godrich produced electronica solo album with Stanley Donwood artwork, and he permitted Colin to program "Guess Again!." It arrived via bundle (it was downloaded a million times in its first week), until a vinyl version arrived in December and a Japanese CD in February. Everyone else had to wait until 2017.

Phil became Philip again for his second solo album, *Weatherhouse*. It was dedicated to Scott Johnson and it was without any Radiohead involvement. It wasn't quite as affecting or effective as *Familial*, but his adult sweetness remained undimmed. Meanwhile, Jonny spent three months in Australia as composer-in-residence with the Australian Chamber Orchestra, and the collaboration's Indian-influenced, nineteen-minute "Water" was premiered in Sydney. He worked with Paul Thomas Anderson once again, this time on the film version of Thomas Pynchon's novel *Inherent Vice*. The soundtrack included Minnie Riperton's wonderful "Les Fleur" and "Spooks," which Radiohead had occasionally played on the *In Rainbows* tour. Jonny rejigged it and enticed two members of the Courtyard-managed Supergrass to play on it. "It's really a half idea we never made work live," Jonny argued. "It's better now than the Pixies/surf pastiche it was." And Phil mentioned that the band were back in the studio.

Both Phil/Philip and Thom would tour their solo work in 2015 (Philip extensively; Thom tentatively) and Jonny returned to India. The previous year he'd worked with Indian-residing Israeli composer Shye Ben Tzur, a man who speaks Urdu and Hebrew. The pair, along with Nigel Godrich and Paul Thomas Anderson, traveled to the hilltop seventeenth-century Mehrangarh Fort in Rajasthan, where *The Jungle Book* and *The Dark Knight Rises* were partly filmed. In this eye-popping setting, they recorded *Junun* with nineteen Indian musicians and an accompanying fifty-four-minute documentary. It's an extraordinarily joyful, accessible collaboration, the sound of Jonny pushing his own boundaries as keenly as he pushes Radiohead's, but with the Indians providing musical ballast.

A MOON SHAPED POOL

RECORDED AT La Fabrique, Saint-Rémy-de-Provence; RAK, London

PRODUCED by Nigel Godrich & Radiohead

PERSONNEL
Colin Greenwood
Ed O'Brien
Jonny Greenwood
Phil Selway
Thom Yorke

COVER ART
Stanley Donwood & Doktor Tchock

RELEASED May 8, 2016
(self-release) & Jun 17, 2016
(XL Recordings)

LABEL XL Recordings, XLCD790

HIGHEST CHART POSITION ON RELEASE UK 1, US 3, FRA 5,
NZ 2, CAN 2, SWI 1, AUS 2, ITA 2,
GER 3, SPA 6, NL 2

TRACK LIST
Burn the Witch
Daydreaming
Decks Dark
Desert Island Disk
Ful Stop
Glass Eyes
Identikit
The Numbers
Present Tense
Tinker Tailor Soldier Sailor Rich Man
    Poor Man Beggar Man Thief
True Love Waits

"An album of nightmare lullabies." NEW YORK TIMES

"Westerners can be too wary to make anything that captures the real roughness of this music, especially the way the brass bands play when they're following processions and weddings down backstreets," argued Jonny to *IndieWire*. "People miss the point of Indian music when they don't hear the tension, excitement or passion: we were just responding to that. We did lots of the singing with the singers holding microphones: it was a little bit hip-hop, actually."

There was more. On August 15, 2015, with Thom safely in Japan playing a *Tomorrow's Modern Boxes* show and Rachel Owen holidaying with Noah and Agnes Mair, a statement was snuck out: "Rachel and I have separated. After 23 highly creative and happy years, for various reasons we have gone our separate ways. It's perfectly amicable and has been common knowledge for some time."

Predictably, the shutters were slammed down vis-à-vis the "various reasons" and Radiohead returned to the studio. Then James Bond tripped them up. Having covered "Nobody Does It Better" on their R.E.M. support, the band were asked to contribute the theme to the forthcoming James Bond film, *Spectre*. At first, they attempted to fob the producers off with "Man of War"—aka "Big Boots (Man-O-War)"—which hadn't made *The Avengers* soundtrack all those years ago. The band had rejected it back then, and now the Bond people concurred. Now Radiohead offered "Spectre," a gorgeous, orchestral ballad, the downbeat cousin of A-ha's John Barry-assisted Bond masterwork "The Living Daylights." Once again, the men from Bond said "No." Too dark, apparently, although precisely what they were expecting from a Radiohead song called "Spectre" remains unclear. Nigel Godrich was furious: "It threw us a massive curveball. It was a real waste of energy. We stopped the album to concentrate on that, since we were told it was going to come to fruition."

"We have," declared Jonny ominously, "changed our method." What he meant was that Thom had changed his method. Thom had played

"The Numbers," "Present Tense," and "Desert Island Disk" solo, but now he was calling for more band input. Nigel Godrich whisked them away to yet another old building, this time the residential studio La Fabrique, a nineteenth-century mill near Nimes which once made fabric pigment. British poet Adam Thorpe described it for *Esquire*: "a sunlit suite of rooms with antique rugs, ornate fireplaces, and elegant period furniture, lined with books in wooded cabinets and invaded by recording equipment."

"It felt hard to make progress," Jonny admitted to *Rolling Stone*. "We just needed some isolation. We operate on a steady diet of anxiety, uncertainty and utter conviction in the songs."

There was further tragedy. Nigel Godrich's sixty-nine-year-old father, Vic Godrich, to whom *A Moon Shaped Pool* would be dedicated, died as they recorded the London Contemporary Orchestra's string section cameo on "Burn the Witch" in London: "I left him on a fucking table in my house and went to record. It was a very, very emotional day for me. He was a string player as well, so it was one of those things where it felt like he would want me to go and do this."

After the best part of two years, the album was finished in the best part of two weeks, and with Thom now Doktor Tchock on the rather will-this-do? artwork, *A Moon Shaped Pool* was rushed out in May 2016, a month after the back catalog was acquired by XL. EMI's *Best Of* and lavish reissues were instantly deleted.

The album pulls together three strands. Nigel Godrich claimed he "put it all together myself," which seems peculiar given the band's hands-on approach and the joke of having the running order determined by (of all things) the alphabet. Certainly, Jonny assumed more musical control, helming the strings and orchestral arrangements which dominated a Radiohead album like no other. Then there was Thom, now without a partner in life. When he declared "as my world comes crashing down" and "careful my love/half of my life" (albeit in reverse), he may well have been thinking of his domestic situation. It would be absurd if he wasn't. On the other hand, such thoughts are hardly out of context since *The Bends* and, anyway, very few lyrics were written after the split. Or, to be more precise, after the announcement of the split . . .

Insistent and breathless, "Burn the Witch" began with an onslaught of upbeat strings not a million miles away from Coldplay's "Viva La Vida" and an accompanying electro drone. It had been on the back burner for over a decade and, unusually, those strings were starting point rather than decoration. "I finally had the gall to say, 'Let's leave this unfinished and let the strings finish it,'" said Jonny. "In the past, I wouldn't have had the brass neck." Quietly, less dramatically than in previous lives, another Radiohead was emerging.

The album's longest track, "Daydreaming," was, according to Thom, the moment at which the new sound began to blossom. If one song concerns the split—"the damage is done"—it's probably this beautiful piano ballad, packed to the gunwales with cellos. Thom had never sounded quite so nakedly vulnerable and it would become his favorite *A Moon Shaped Pool* moment.

"Decks Dark" talks of spacecraft, but before it ends in a jagged swirl. There are haunting choral voices, tinkling piano, a rare overt sighting of Phil's drums and a grooving bassline. A most underrated diversion on a most underrated album.

Thom had played "Desert Island Disk" in a solo acoustic show in Paris in 2015, but in band format it's Jonny's most Ry Cooder moment since "Hunting Bears." The title isn't in the lyric, but its gleefully bitter tone is a reminder of British Prime Minister David Cameron's 2006 appearance on the Radio 4 program *Desert Island Discs*, thirteen years before Thom joined him. David Cameron selected "Fake Plastic Trees" as one of his eight pieces of music to take to a mythical desert island. That the Conservative chose R.E.M.'s "Perfect Circle," too, added vicarious fury.

An occasional live treat since 2012, "Ful Stop" (never "Full Stop") marked Clive Deamer's Radiohead studio debut, although it's hardly a festival of percussion. Instead, it's a trip back to the Can years and it's propelled by an electrobeat similar to both Kraftwerk's "Trans-Europe Express" and David Bowie's "Station to Station." Jonny loved the mildly bonkers ending. He was right. Being Jonny, he usually is.

The glacier-paced "Glass Eyes" is another of Thom's traumatic journey songs and, once again, he sounds broken to leave the womb of yet another train to enter the wider, colder world. As has been the case since *Pablo Honey*, he is a man in need of a hug. Aren't we all?

Another refugee from *The King of Limbs* tour, there was an attempt to record "Identikit" at Jack White's Third Man studios in Nashville in 2012—unsuccessful sessions over which omertà has descended—with little success, bar providing a rough template. Its dual vocal lines showed that, even now, Radiohead could break new ground, but its sparse, echo-laden feel makes it more of a Thom solo track.

Formerly known as "Silent Spring," the exquisite "The Numbers" was performed by Thom solo in Paris. Always intended as a band song, he pointed to the moment Jonny's guitar kicks in and admitted such wonders were beyond him. The first half was their most "Albatross" moment since "House of Cards," the second half soaring, jarringly jaunty, strings-fueled yacht rock.

"Present Tense" had been knocking around in one form or another since 2002, sometimes with a "The" in the title. A simple guitar song in its inchoate phase, on *A Moon Shaped Pool* it was a satisfying marriage of subtle strings, Thom in his intermittently resurrected crooner mode, hi-hat shuffle, and a reminder that Ennio Morricone's influence had not wholly withered.

The Radiohead song with the longest title, "Tinker Tailor Soldier Sailor Rich Man Poor Man Beggar Man Thief" would be the first on *A*

Moon Shaped Pool to be jettisoned from the live set. With good reason.

As we know, Nigel Godrich had described Thom's solo version of "True Love Waits" on *I Might Be Wrong: Live Recordings* as "shitty." Twenty-one years after its first live airing, and something of a holy grail for the cognoscenti, the gorgeous *A Moon Shaped Pool* version made Nigel Godrich's point for him. Still stripped down, still adapting "You're not living, you're just killing time," the central quote from Ray Bradbury's *Fahrenheit 451*, Thom's voice cracked over a deep, intricate arrangement. Perhaps post-Rachel Owen, its lyric had added resonance. Or perhaps not: Once again it was swiftly dumped from the live set, shortly after "Tinker Tailor Soldier Sailor Rich Man Poor Man Beggar Man Thief."

Like everything since *OK Computer*, *A Moon Shaped Pool* divided opinion, but what *The New York Times* argued was "an album of nightmare lullabies" was in fact Radiohead at their most yearning, even if the jerry-built running order does it no artistic favors. As *Rolling Stone* rightly noted, "The magic is in the blending."

Not only was Cillian Murphy a force behind getting Radiohead's music onto *Peaky Blinders*, he offered a shrewd appraisal of *A Moon Shaped Pool*, too: "It's just absolutely beautiful. I've been listening to it on repeat. We've lost the art of listening to albums these days. This demands to be listened to as a whole. You only get a band like Radiohead every generation."

"It felt hard to make progress. We just needed some isolation. We operate on a steady diet of anxiety, uncertainty and utter conviction in the songs." JONNY

The opening night of Thom's "Tomorrow's Modern Boxes Tour" at the Franklin Music Hall, Philadelphia, PA, USA, 23 November, 2018.

12

WE HAVE BECOME VERY ADEPT AT BEING RADIOHEAD

Twelve days after *A Moon Shaped Pool*'s release, like greyhounds out of the traps, Radiohead were on the road again. For a while, the new songs were sprinkled throughout the set, in album running order. Thom wept in Paris after "Nude"; Flea saw their set at the Outside Lands Festival in San Francisco and announced it had changed his life; and when the tour's first leg finished in Austin, Texas, in October 2016, Jonny prepared to take *Junun* on the road (now named after the album, the band Junun would actually support Radiohead the following year). All looked rosy. It wasn't.

A week before Christmas 2016, Rachel Owen died of cancer, aged just forty-eight. Again, there was nothing to say; again, nothing would be said. Following on from the gratis 2008 release of *In Rainbows* stems (i.e. separate instrumental tracks) to "Nude" and "Reckoner," which remixers could use as they pleased, in February they had given away a "groove pack" which allowed aspiring imitators to add everything but the beats from all Radiohead material to their own songs. By the time the tour reconvened in Miami in March, Thom openly had a new girlfriend, Dajana Roncione, a Sicilian actor sixteen years his junior who wasn't averse to displays of public affection and who had discreetly joined the tour the previous summer. In June, "Creep" was played at Glastonbury and the same month also saw the beautifully packaged *OK Computer OKNOTOK 1997 2017*, the first reissue with band involvement. Dedicated to Rachel Owen, it comprised a remixed *OK Computer*, a slew of B-sides, and three unreleased songs from the era.

They finally felt sufficiently secure to restore the long-lost "Lift" to its natural home.

To celebrate, they made a video for "Lift." Helmed by skate director Oscar Hudson, it was loosely based around Marc Isaacs's 2001 film, *Lift*. It briefly features Dajana Roncione, and Agnes Mair, alongside characters from the "Paranoid Android" and "Karma Police" videos. "We wanted to walk a line with this video," explained Hudson. "Somewhere between not looking back too much without ignoring the history of the song."

"I Promise" might have been the perfect bridge between *The Bends* and *OK Computer*, and when they played it in Oslo in June 2017, it was twenty-one years after its previous live airing. The song now called "Man of War" may not have been good enough for *The Avengers* or James Bond, but it really was both films' loss.

For some of the 2017 leg of the tour, Radiohead were joined by all thirteen of their children and it climaxed with a date in Tel Aviv. Israel was the first country to fall for Radiohead, and Jonny's wife, Sharona Katan, was born there. The show was Radiohead's first in Israel since 2000 and only their eighth ever, but they had to change hotels when Katan's original choice announced the booking. The anti-Israel lobby soon mobilized. Wisely, Jonny kept a low profile. Like a lioness guarding her cub, Thom did not.

"It's deeply disrespectful to assume we're either misinformed or so retarded we can't make these decisions ourselves," he told *Rolling Stone* in response to demands Radiohead should boycott Israel. "It's patronizing in the extreme, it's offensive."

In the same magazine, Roger Waters, late of Pink Floyd, weighed in. "My answer to people who say we should go there, sit around the campfire and sing songs is 'No, we shouldn't'," he thundered. "Anybody who's tempted to do that, like our friends in Radiohead, should educate themselves. I know Thom Yorke's been whining about how he feels insulted, but people are suggesting he doesn't know what's going on."

Thom wrote to Waters's colleague in the anti-Israel BDS (Boycott, Disinvestment & Sanctions) movement, filmmaker Ken Loach, whose films were distributed in Israel:

"Playing in a country isn't the same as endorsing its government. As in America, we've played in Israel for over 20 years through a succession of governments, some more liberal than others. We don't endorse Netanyahu any more than Trump, but we still play in America. Music, art and academia is about crossing borders, not building them; about open minds not closed ones, about shared humanity, dialogue and freedom of expression. I hope that makes it clear, Ken."

Awkwardly, Nigel Godrich had just produced Roger Waters's terrific and terrifically angry *Is This the Life We Really Want?*, but he too chipped in, albeit delicately: "I don't believe in cultural boycotts. I don't think they're positive. The people you'd be denying are those who agree with you, rather than the government. So they're not a good idea. Thom and Roger are peas in a pod in certain respects. They just have a disagreement about this. Thom feels very protective of Jonny, which I completely get, but I'm not in the middle of Thom and Roger."

With Jonny's Junun and Arab-Israeli act Dudu Tassa & The Kuwaitis supporting, the Tel Aviv gig was a mammoth twenty-seven-song spectacular which included "Creep" and Sharona Katan's favorite Radiohead song, "The Bends," aired for only the fourth time since 2009. It was one of the great Radiohead shows. "A lot of stuff has been said about this," shrugged Thom from the Park Hayarkon stage to the 48,500 gathered, "but in the end, we play some music."

Dudu Tassa, who sang in Arabic, would subsequently support Radiohead across North America, a tour during which Jonny checked into hotels as *Curb Your Enthusiasm* character Marty Funkhouser. Afterwards, Dudu Tassa explained the link to *The Jerusalem Post*:

I've known Jonny for 15 years. I met his wife's sister on vacation in northern Israel and they came to one of my shows. From there, we kept in touch. When my first album with The Kuwaitis was released, Jonny really liked what he heard and uploaded our album to Radiohead's website.

Radiohead and their American audience are very experimental people and they connected to our music. That Radiohead gave us a chance to present what we do says something about them. It's not by chance they are one of the world's biggest bands. We never spoke about BDS. They are pro-freedom to create, freedom of choice and unbounded musical expression.

Less controversially, Phil as Philip penned the strings-based soundtrack to the World War II mother-daughter drama *Let Me Go* on which Lamb's Lou Rhodes sang the heart-stopping "Walk." Jonny reunited with Paul Thomas Anderson for the *Phantom Thread* soundtrack, which won an Ivor Novello Award in 2019, the year after it was Oscar-nominated, losing to Alexandre Desplat's *The Shape of Water*. By spooky coincidence, Alexandre Desplat had also soundtracked *The Twilight Saga: New Moon* to which Thom had contributed "Hearing Damage." Jonny would also score British director Lynne Ramsey's dark *You Were Never Really Here*. Thom finished 2017 in the United States playing yet more solo shows.

OK COMPUTER
OKNOTOK 1997 2017

RECORDED at Canned Applause, Didcot; St Catherine's Court, Bath; Abbey Road, London

PRODUCED BY Nigel Godrich & Radiohead

PERSONNEL
Colin Greenwood
Ed O'Brien
Jonny Greenwood
Phil Selway
Thom Yorke

ADDITIONAL PERSONNEL
Royal Philharmonic Orchestra: strings on "Man of War"

COVER ART
Stanley Donwood: pictures
The White Chocolate Farm: pictures

RELEASED Jun 23, 2017

LABEL XL Recordings , XLCD868

HIGHEST CHART POSITION ON RELEASE UK 2, US 23, GER 13, NZ 7, CAN 10, SWI 16, SPA 11, AUS 6

TRACK LIST
OK
Airbag
Paranoid Android
Subterranean Homesick Alien
Exit Music (For a Film)
Let Down
Karma Police
Fitter Happier
Electioneering
Climbing up the Walls
No Surprises
Lucky
The Tourist

NOTOK
I Promise
Man of War
Lift
Lull
Meeting in the Aisle
Melatonin
A Reminder
Polyethylene (Parts 1 & 2)
Pearly
Palo Alto
How I Made My Millions

"Somewhere between not looking back too much without ignoring the history." OSCAR HUDSON

In 2018, there were South and North American *A Moon Shaped Pool* dates for Radiohead, big dates. Perhaps now, more than ever, it's worth pausing to note that long after any novelty value has worn off, this uncommercial, cussed, wonderful band were still filling arenas and still had the commercial clout to fill Madison Square Garden for four nights.

Jonny, the band member who had been most traumatized by Radiohead's move from clubs to arenas had, at last, come to terms with life in a glasshouse. "One of the great joys of playing American sports arenas is their amazing communal showers. I'll get to the venue early, seek out those rooms that smell of Deep Heat and jockstraps, get out my recorder, play one of Telemann's canonic sonatas and be swamped in this flattering reverb." He may have been joking of course.

Thom toured solo again, this time across Europe, before releasing *Suspiria* in October 2018. The soundtrack to Luca Guadagnino's horror flick was mostly composed before the film was shot. As a reminder of how quickly the years had passed, Noah, the boy to whom Thom had read *Bagpuss* stories, played drums on "Has Ended" and "Volk."

There were smatterings of band maneuvers. Having been unsuccessfully nominated for the Rock and Roll Hall of Fame in 2017, Radiohead were nominated again in 2018 and finally inducted in March 2019. Thom claimed to be too busy to attend, while outing himself as a Billie Eilish fan ("Because she's being herself, people are really into it"), but when pressed he was unsurprisingly ambivalent. "We've always been blasé about that stuff. We don't want to offend anyone, we just don't understand it."

They were inducted by "Radio Head" writer David Byrne, who lauded "the quality and constant innovation in their music" and "the innovations in how they release their work, market it and get it to the public."

Ed and Phil did turn up. Phil was especially gracious:

I'd like to say a little bit about what being in Radiohead means to me. It can be awkward and challenging, but that's what's kept us all interested for the past three decades. I'm beyond proud of what the five of us have achieved and I can easily place myself back in my first band rehearsal at school: that band is still very recognizable to me, whenever we play. We've learned our musical chops together. Each new song has been a lesson and our albums act as a chart of that learning process. We may not be the greatest musicians and we're certainly not the most media-friendly, but we have become very adept at being Radiohead. When that connects with people, it feels amazing. I'd never take any of this for granted, so thank you, thank you so much.

In April, there was a new Thom song, "Gawpers" and a classical composition "Don't Fear the Light," both of which premiered in Paris. Sisters Katia and Marielle Labèque played pianos, while Thom wailed, most seductively.

Indeed, Thom claimed to already be thinking about life after Radiohead, telling *Blender* that after finishing the band's last ever concert with Neil Young's "Fuckin' Up," rather than count his estimated £24 million fortune and wonder how a band this bold, this brave, this singular had sold over 30 million albums, he had plans. "I'll age badly. Follow random pathways in the forest. Smoke a pipe. Become a hermit. Never shave again. Take ecstasy at weekends. Develop a Valium habit. Read the Bible. Go to Tibet. Become an MP. Change my name. Laugh at economists. Start skanking dancefloor style."

The truth though is that Thom Yorke just can't stop. In June 2019 he released the Carl Jung-influenced *Anima* ("soul" in Dajana Roncione's Italian), another Nigel Godrich-produced electro solo album with Stanley Donwood artwork. This time, though, Thom permitted Phil to play "sped-up" drums on "Impossible Knots." As Danny Eccleston perceptively noted in *Mojo*: "He has been an electronica artist of sorts for five years longer than he was primarily a rock singer and there are still those hoping he'll snap out of it."

Paul Thomas Anderson had directed the video to *A Moon Shaped Pool*'s "Daydreaming," but he was usually Jonny's collaborator. Yet as *Amina* hurtled its way to the top of the US Dance/Electronic chart, Thom worked with the director to make a 15-minute film to accompany the album, streamed on Netflix. A visual feast starring Thom and featuring Dajana Roncione, plus a host of nodding dancers on the Prague subway, there were abandoned briefcases, the whiff of an Ismail Kadare novel and a lovers' reconciliation in Paris. Impressively, Paul Thomas Anderson's command to Thom: "More Buster Keaton" makes more sense in practice than theory.

Bafflingly to those who had seen him wilt during *The Bends* and *OK Computer* dates, Thom toured it extensively, alongside Nigel Godrich and visual artist Tarik Barri, his live collaborators since 2015. They'd sometimes finish with "Like Spinning Plates." And Thom still found time for "Daily Battles," a lovely piano-based song with Flea (the childhood trumpeter was on brass rather than bass) for the film *Motherless Brooklyn*.

During the month of *Amina*'s release, Radiohead were blackmailed. Hackers stole *OK Computer* recordings from Thom's MiniDisc archive.

Payment of $150,000 would have secured the tapes' return. Instead, the band sold all eighteen hours (they must have made copies) on Bandcamp for £18 over 18 days as MiniDisc [Hacked] and gave the profits to environmental campaign group Extinction Rebellion. "It was never intended for public consumption, it's only tangentially interesting and very, very long. Rainy out, isn't it though. . ." chuckled Jonny. It's hard to argue with him, but one of the nine versions of "Lift" is definitive (why it failed to make even *OK Computer OKNOTOK 1997 2017* must remain a mystery). There are lost songs including "Attenzione!" and "When I Get Bored Give Me One of Those." There is a proper band version of "True Love Waits" (why they persisted with Thom-centric versions must remain another mystery). There are too many solo Thom demos and there is a whopping twelve-minute "Paranoid Android," but sometimes too much light hides the magic.

If the roadhog *Amina* dates were a surprise, Thom's September appearance on *Desert Island Discs*, a BBC radio institution since 1942, was a game changer. Guests such as alleged Radiohead/R.E.M. fan David Cameron are questioned sympathetically, but in return those guests are expected to reveal something of themselves and buy into the concept of being stranded on a desert island with eight pieces of music, a book, and a luxury.

Many credited Dajana Roncione's influence, but amazingly all the same, Thom was a willing castaway who adhered to the rules. He cheerily shared details (vague details, but for a man who had never acknowledged being married to Rachel Owen, details all the same) of his life. The frequent flyer admitted to climate change hypocrisy and he even spoke, beautifully, about Owen's passing and his parenting of motherless children: "I'm more like their friend. I can't hope to be their mum, but we're alright. I'm a relaxed dad, but they would argue differently. I'm really proud and I can't believe they're anything to do with me. They're such great people."

And he spoke of his real ambition: "When the kids' mum died, it was a very difficult period, we went through a lot. She suffered a great deal. My ambition is to make sure we've come out of it alright. I have a new partner who's brought light into it. If all that's OK, then I want to tinker away, making music, taking risks: it's more than I can ask for, it's way more than I need."

If appearing on the program was one of the most unThom things he'd ever done, his musical selections were very Thom indeed:

His new friends, the Labèque Sisters' version of Maurice Ravel's "Le Jardin Féerique" ("The Fairy Garden"). "It flowers like the dawn to me."

Scott Walker's "It's Raining Today." "Whimsical, but so profound musically. I'll put it on when it rains on the island."

Talking Heads' "Born Under Punches (The Heat Goes On)," Thom's choice if he was only allowed one song. "*Remain in Light* was like a bomb going off in my head. Even now it's not like anything else."

Aphex Twin/Squarepusher's "Freeman, Hardy & Willis Acid." "It's so intense, really vicious. It harkens to a period I'd missed because I'd decided to be in a rock band. It was a door opening to me."

Neil Young's "After the Gold Rush." "I'm going to be on my own on this desert island, so I'm going to need voices that have really helped me."

R.E.M.'s "Talk About the Passion." "There's a joy and a madness to it. They were the link between the art student me and the musician me. Michael Stipe was my hero and now I'm friends with him. When people started treating me like Jesus, I'd call him and he'd help."

Sidney Bechet's "Blue Horizon." "This is incredibly sexy to me, so so sexual."

Nina Simone's "Lilac Wine." "I'm into having a bit of time to chill, but my heart is going to need help. This has affected me in a way that few pieces of music have. She made it dark, light, fragile and on the edge of crazy. I need her on a desert island."

His book was *Zen Mind, Beginner's Mind*, a compilation of Shunryu Suzuki's teachings. His luxury item was a tape recorder, which he soon upgraded to a recording studio.

Jonny too was still spreading his wings. The same months he debuted "Horror Vacui," his 36-minute piece for 68 strings to close a BBC Prom he'd curated, which also featured music from Krzysztof Penderecki, Steve Reich, and Heinrich Ignaz Franz Biber. On the back of his BBC Prom, Jonny announced Octatonic, a label devoted to his own and others' classical music.

"I'm only recording soloists or small groups," he explained. "As it's my party, I'm including some of my ideas that have never been recorded. I want to produce great, intimate recordings, which capture the music in a way that does justice to the musicians' talent and the composers they interpret."

Ed finally completed *Earth*, his Flood and Catherine Marks produced, Alan Moulder-mixed, solo album. Laura Marling and Phil/Philip's drummer Glenn Kotche guested, and Ed re-christened himself EOB. Mostly conceived during the O'Brien family's year in Brazil, *Earth* was recorded in Wales and London during 2018 and released in April 2020. The first offering, "Santa Teresa," was a moody, sculpted instrumental in the vein of Trent Reznor's soundtrack work, but it only made the album as a bonus track in Japan. The second, "Brasil" was anchored by Colin's bass, the only song on which a bandmate appeared. The nine-minute epic began as an acoustic strum and expanded into a controlled maelstrom. Two months before *Earth*'s release, Ed played four low-key dates in Toronto, Chicago, New York and Los Angeles, during which he covered erstwhile Tangerine Dreamer Ulrich Schnauss's "On My Own". A much longer tour was booked, but Covid-19 scuppered that, and the project was sapped of all momentum. "I'm not going my own way, it's additional to Radiohead, very much in tandem with them," he told the BBC. In April he announced, he "most probably" had caught Covid.

Whatever surprises loomed, they were postponed—or perhaps abandoned—by the global pandemic. The UK went into lockdown on 20 March 2020. As we know, Ed was the first casualty, both personally and professionally, but Radiohead as a unit went on hold, although "now that you have no choice whether or not you fancy a quiet night in," they released a past concert a week on their YouTube channel. In September, Thom married Dajana Roncione in Sicily. The happy couple even released a photograph to celebrate.

That doesn't mean they stopped working. Thom, Jonny and Sons of Kemet drummer Tom Skinner formed a new band, The Smile, titled after a Ted Hughes poem which may or may not allude to Christ's crucifixion. They debuted at the virtual Glastonbury of 2021, playing from Worthy Farm itself. "We're not ha-ha, more the smile of the guy who lies to you every day," said Thom to his invisible audience. They sounded like a more restrained Radiohead and "Thin Thing" was rather fantastic. They even had a go at "Skirting on the Surface," which Thom had played during his acoustic interludes during Atoms For Peace shows and which Radiohead had briefly dabbled with on the *King of Limbs* tour. Nigel Godrich produced an album.

Jonny had other projects too. In November 2021, two of his soundtracks appeared simultaneously. *Spencer*, a fictionalized account of the dying days of the marriage between Princess Diana—formerly Diana Spencer—and Prince Charles. Jonny's work was a spiraling mixture of avant baroque ("Calling the Whipper In," the thrilling "Invention for Harpsichord & Compression") and mournful bass ("Arrival").

The Power of the Dog, the Jane Campion-directed film of Thomas Savage's novel, saw plucked strings on "25 Years" and crazy, super-speed piano on "Detuned Mechanical Piano." Needless to say, no Western has ever had accompaniment quite like this. It might just be Jonny's best soundtrack work. The film starred Benedict Cumberbatch, with whom

Jonny and Thom had established a friendship after they saw his *Hamlet* at London's Barbican in 2015. Cumberbatch mused upon the prospect of him starring in an unlikely Radiohead biopic: "I don't think they want their lives made into a film. It would be quite a weird film, love them as I do. Not at the moment, but we'll see. Watch this space."

In January 2022, Jonny re-convened yet again with director Paul Thomas Anderson to score the musical cues for the '70s coming-of-age comedy *Licorice Pizza* and provide the lovely, lilting instrumental title track.

In February 2021, Colin wrote an opinion piece for *The Guardian*, detailing the myriad problems Brexit had caused touring musicians: "as a musician who wants to jump on the Eurostar and go play, my heart sinks at all the new costs and kerfuffle and I'm lucky enough to afford it."

Phil, meanwhile, appeared on a BBC documentary, *On the Road with Independent Venue Week*, where he extolled the virtues of independent music venues. He even appeared on a panel to discuss the film.

Reassuringly there was movement on the band front. *Kid A* and *Amnesiac* had been recorded at the same time around the turn of the century. In November 2021, 21 years after *Kid A*'s release, the pair were re-released together as *Kid A Mnesia*. The originals sounded astonishing then and they sound astonishing now, but the real bonus was less that it reached four in the UK and 12 in the US, more the accompanying third album *Kid A Mnesia*.

Kid A Mnesia featured two (sort of) new tracks. "If You Say the Word," which had been called "C-Minor Song" and then "Say the Word" during the *Kid A/Amnesiac* sessions. They were never happy with it until now. The spectacularly dark "Follow me Around" was even older. They began it during the *OK Computer* sessions, tried it again while recording *Kid A/Amnesiac* and, giving the people what they want, played it live after hard-core fans heard some of it on "Meeting People is Easy" and established a now-defunct website (followmearound.com) to demand it.

Elsewhere, there were snatches from the sessions and alternative versions, notably "How to Disappear into Strings," the instrumental take on "How to Disappear Completely." Radiohead still cared about their past. As *Classic Rock* perceptively noted, "Radiohead's loving tending of their back catalog wins out again." For just £185 ($247), you could buy an accompanying tea set made from fine bone china, decorated with *Kid A Mnesia* art. There were bedsheets and tins of biscuits available too.

Speaking of accompaniments, there was an exhibition, also titled *Kid A Mnesia*, a collaboration between Thom, Stanley Donwood and Nigel Godrich. Originally meant as a physical installation, it was reduced to online by the pandemic. Even so, it was a sense tickling affair. Packed with Stanley Donwood landscapes and soundtracked by shards of *Kid A* and *Amnesiac* material, despite Thom's protestations, this collaboration with Epic Games certainly had the air of a computer game. There were walls, boxes, aliens, the peaks of the Kid A sleeve and, of course, bears. Online or not, it was an extraordinary immersive experience.

In January 2019, long before the pandemic, the venerable warriors had quietly reconvened. Just for a chat. A long, long time afterwards, Ed said a little, without really saying anything: "we've got some stuff we were talking about, but I'm going to be particularly vague. It could be next year; it could be 10 years' time. The important thing is that when we get together, it's not because we should or because we ought, but because we really want to."

In truth, they've never done it any other way, but there's one last thing. They're in their fourth decade, their lineup remains unbroken, yet the feeling that this is a band on the edge has never evaporated. As Thom says, "You've got to be prepared to torch it at any moment." They've always had a lighter to hand.

"The important thing is that when we get together, it's not because we should or because we ought, but because we really want to." PHIL

ACKNOWLEDGMENTS AND SOURCES

Thanks to Ian Gittins for playing cupid and to Rob Nichols for being the editor I'd always hoped for. This is for Michelle, Jessica and Oscar: everything's for them, really.

MAGAZINES AND NEWSPAPERS: *The Age, The Big Issue, Billboard, Blender, Classic Rock, Curfew, Daily Record, Dazed & Confused, The Guardian, Ha'ir, The Irish Times, The Jerusalem Post, Juice, Melody Maker, Mojo, Mondo Sonoro, New Musical Express, Option, Q Magazine, Raygun, Rolling Stone, Rotherham Advertiser, Select, Spin, The Sunday Times, Time Out, The Times, Volume, Vox, Wire, Wisden Cricket Monthly, Oxford Times, The Spectator*

TV, RADIO AND WEBSITES: Abingdon School (https://www.abingdon.org. uk/), *Addicted To Noise* (http://a2noise.com/), BBC Radio 1, BBC Radio 4, BBC 6 Music, *Citizen Insane* (https://citizeninsane.eu/), *Dead Air Space* (http://www.radiohead. com/deadairspace/2019061), *Discovering Radiohead* (3DD Productions), *IndieWire* (https://www.indiewire.com/page/2/), *MTV*, Rudi Enos Design (http://www.rudi-enosdesign.com), Standlake School (http://standlakeschool.co.uk/), *Top of the Pops.*

BOOKS

Aizlewood, John: *Love is the Drug*; Penguin, 1994
Clarke, Martin: *Radiohead: Hysterical & Useless*; Plexus, 2010
Doheny, James: *Radiohead: The Stories Behind Every Song*; Carlton, 2002
Loxley, Robert; Witcomb Gerald; Rowe, Gavin: *Bridges (Ladybird Leaders)*;
    Ladybird, 1974
Malins, Steve: *Radiohead, Coming Up For Air*; Virgin, 1997
Randall, Mac: *Exit Music: The Radiohead Story*; Omnibus, 2011
Egan, Jennifer: *Manhattan Beach*; Corsair, 2017

PICTURE CREDITS
Picture Insert 1t: Matt Anker/Retna; 1b: Ian Patrick/Retna; 2t: Bob Berg/Avalon; 2b: Michael Putland/Getty; 3t: Roger Sargent/Shutterstock; 3b: Cuccagna/Dalle/ Retna; 4t: Frank Micelotta/Getty; 4b: Nitin Vadukul/Avalon; 5t: Lucy Nicholson/ Getty; 5b: Theo Wargo/WireImage/Getty; 6t: Leslie McGhie/WireImage/Getty; 6b: Kevin Nixon/Classic Rock Magazine/Shutterstock; 7t: Scott Applewhite/ AP/Shutterstock; 7b: Christian Bertrand/Alamy; 8t: Evan Agostini/Invision/AP/ Shutterstock; 8b: Daniele Baldi/Alamy
Interior 4: Alexander Kenney/Alamy; 6: Cuccagna/Dalle/Retna; 26: Idols/Avalon; 36: Monfourny/Dalle/Avalon; 52, 72: Pat Pope/Shutterstock; 90: Photoshot/Retna/ Avalon; 100: Nitin Vadukul/Avalon; 126: Robin Francois/Avalon; 142: Mick Hutson/ Redferns/Getty; 154: RUSSO/Dalle/Retna; 164: Mediapunch/Shutterstock; 176: Erik Kabik/Media Punch/Alamy